Home Office Research Study 224

Drug misuse declared in 2000: results from the British Crime Survey

Malcolm Ramsay, Paul Baker, Chris Goulden, Clare Sharp and Arun Sondhi

The views expressed in this report are those of the authors, not necessarily those of the Home Office (nor do they reflect Government policy).

Home Office Research, Development and Statistics Directorate
September 2001

Home Office Research Studies

The Home Office Research Studies are reports on research undertaken by or on behalf of the Home Office. They cover the range of subjects for which the Home Secretary has responsibility. Other publications produced by the Research, Development and Statistics Directorate include Findings, Statistical Bulletins and Statistical Papers.

The Research, Development and Statistics Directorate

RDS is part of the Home Office. The Home Office's purpose is to build a safe, just and tolerant society in which the rights and responsibilities of individuals, families and communities are properly balanced and the protection and security of the public are maintained.

RDS is also a part of the Government Statistical Service (GSS). One of the GSS aims is to inform Parliament and the citizen about the state of the nation and provide a window on the work and performance of government, allowing the impact of government policies and actions to be assessed.

Therefore -

Research Development and Statistics Directorate exists to improve policy making, decision taking and practice in support of the Home Office purpose and aims, to provide the public and Parliament with information necessary for informed debate and to publish information for future use.

First published 2001
Application for reproduction should be made to the Communications and Development Unit, Room 201, Home Office, 50 Queen Anne's Gate, London SW1H 9AT.
© Crown copyright 2001   ISBN 1 84082 701 7
                           ISSN 0072 6435

Foreword

The British Crime Survey (BCS) has been used for a number of years to estimate the prevalence of drug use among the general population in England and Wales. It has a vital role to play in tracking the progress of the young people's targets in the Government's anti-drugs strategy. The results of the 2000 survey enable us to see what progress has been made against the baseline rates published in the report on the drugs component of the 1998 BCS.

The main findings from the 2000 survey show no significant increases in the proportion of young people under 25 using cocaine, heroin or Class A drugs since 1998. Some encouraging news is that overall drug use among teenagers has fallen significantly from 1994 levels. However, there has been a significant rise in the proportion of teenagers using cocaine.

From 2001 onwards, the BCS will be carried out on an annual basis with a considerably larger sample size (including a booster sample of young people). This will help to ensure more effective monitoring of the Government's ten-year strategy for tackling drug misuse.

DAVID PYLE
Drugs and Alcohol Research Unit
Research, Development and Statistics Directorate

Acknowledgements

The authors would like to thank Eileen Goddard (Office for National Statistics) and Lana Harrison (Centre for Drug and Alcohol Studies, University of Delaware, US) for acting as independent assessors for this report.

Thanks are also due to present and former colleagues in the British Crime Survey team for their advice and assistance concerning data and statistical issues and to other colleagues who have provided help from the Drugs and Alcohol Research Unit and the rest of the Research, Development and Statistics Directorate at the Home Office.

The National Centre for Social Research and the Social Survey Division of the Office for National Statistics are gratefully acknowledged for carrying out the survey fieldwork, as are the authors of the accompanying British Crime Survey 2000 technical report (Jon Hales, Lynne Henderson, Debbie Collins and Harriet Becher).

Malcolm Ramsay
Paul Baker
Chris Goulden
Clare Sharp
Arun Sondhi

Contents

Summary

The extent of illicit drug misuse in Britain continues to be an area of keen interest for Government policy, the media and the public into the 21st century, as it was throughout the 1990s. In 2000, the primary means of measuring the broad extent of drug misuse among the general population, and of young adults in particular, remains the British Crime Survey (BCS). This is a large-scale and high quality survey, with a core sample representative of households in England and Wales. There was also a booster sample of respondents from visible ethnic minority groups.

The BCS included an almost identical drugs self-report component in each of four sweeps, carried out in 1994, 1996, 1998 and 2000. This component asks whether interviewees, aged 16 to 59, have taken any of the most commonly used drugs in their lifetime, the last year and last month. This report focuses on the broad group of young adults (aged 16 to 29) and on drug use within the previous year, as this combination is thought to provide a good balance providing sufficient numbers for analysis yet having relevance to comparatively recent trends.

The Government's anti-drugs strategy hones in further on the 16 to 24 age group and particularly on their use of Class A drugs within the last year and last month. Ambitious targets have been set for reductions in the extent of drug use by a quarter by 2005 and a half by 2008, from the baselines set in the last BCS drugs report for 1998. The 2000 BCS therefore provides the first opportunity to assess whether these essential outcome measures of the strategy are potentially 'on track' or not. These assessments can be found in detail in the final chapter of this report (Chapter 5), although synopses of this and the four preceding chapters follow in this summary.

Introduction (Chapter 1)

This report is the fourth in a series presenting the latest figures on drug use for the general population of England and Wales in 2000, the three previous reports being based on surveys carried out in 1994, 1996 and 1998. The BCS is the official monitoring instrument for the 'young people' key target in the Government's anti-drugs strategy for 16- to 24-year-olds, sitting alongside a complementary schools survey for those aged 11 to 15. There are powerful advantages to 'piggybacking' the drugs component onto the BCS, which is primarily a survey of victimisation, but also drawbacks, including the potential for under-reporting of drug use.

When other surveys of drug use in the UK, most of them carried out in schools, are considered, no clear-cut message emerges. In England, there were some indications of reductions in use in the late 1990s but on the other hand, surveys sponsored by the Department of Health point if anything to increases in prevalence from 1998. None of the different surveys demonstrate any substantial growth in levels of drug use.

Current patterns of drug use (Chapter 2)

The main findings from the 2000 BCS were:

- Around a third of those aged 16 to 59 had tried drugs in their lifetime. However, the proportions using drugs in the last year and last month were much lower at 11 per cent and six per cent respectively.
- Rates of use of 'any drug' were generally higher in young people; the figures for 16- to 29-year-olds were 50 per cent for lifetime use, 25 per cent for use in the last year and 16 per cent for use in the last month.
- Men were more likely to report the use of drugs than women. Men aged between 16 and 59 were 1.4 times more likely than women in this age group to have tried drugs in their lifetime. The gender gap widens with more recent use; the equivalent ratios are 1.8 for use in the last year and 2.3 for use in the last month.
- Cannabis was the most commonly used drug, with just over a fifth of young people aged 16 to 29 reporting use within the last year.
- Heroin use remained low at around one per cent of 16- to 29-year-olds using it within the last year. However, cocaine use was more common, with five per cent of this age group reporting use within the last year – a level similar to ecstasy.
- About a fifth of young people have used Class A drugs in their lifetime (typically including ecstasy and/or cocaine); the proportion using Class A drugs in the last year and last month was considerably lower at eight per cent and four per cent respectively.

This chapter also examines regional, socio-economic and lifestyle factors. The key results are listed:

- Prevalence rates for particular drugs varied considerably by region, with London having consistently higher rates than other regions for any drug, Class A drugs, cocaine and ecstasy.
- An analysis of different types of residential neighbourhoods (ACORN) showed uniformly higher levels of drug use among 16 to 29s living in affluent urban areas for 'any drug', cocaine and Class A drugs.
- Although drug use was found not to vary significantly between income groups for most drug types, the rate for heroin was notably higher in the poorest income group (3% compared with less than 0.5% in the intermediate and richest groups). Similar patterns were found when education, social class and employment status were examined, whereby the use of drugs in general (and use of cocaine in particular) was relatively widespread across the population but heroin use was more associated with the less affluent groups.
- Single people and those living in rented accommodation were more likely to have taken drugs. Drug use was also more common for those who visited pubs and clubs and drank alcohol more frequently.
- Population estimates show that, of the nine and a half million young people aged 16 to 29 in England and Wales, at least 2.3 million would have used a prohibited drug in the last year.

Changing patterns of drug use, 1994 to 2000 (Chapter 3)

This chapter examines changes in the extent of drug use over the four comparable sweeps of the BCS in 1994, 1996, 1998 and 2000, mainly in relation to use within the last year among 16- to 29-year-olds and related sub-groups according to region, ACORN category and employment status. The main findings include:

- Continued (but possibly decelerating) growth in cocaine use across all age ranges, including the youngest group in the BCS, the 16- to 19-year-olds, where use of cocaine in the last year increased from one per cent in 1994 to four per cent in 2000.
- Declines in the use of some other drugs, most notably amphetamine, which fell by almost a half among 16- to 29-year-olds from levels in 1996–1998, but also LSD and poppers. Use of 'any drug' in the last year by 16- to 19-year-olds fell from around a third in 1994 to just over a quarter by 2000.
- A continuation of very low reported levels of heroin use across all age ranges and both sexes.

- Broad stability in use of ecstasy since 1996, although levels were significantly higher among 25- to 29-year-old men in 2000 than in any previous survey.
- Young men experienced the greatest fluctuations in levels of drug use, in terms of increases and decreases, across the four sweeps of the BCS.
- Although London has always had the highest rates of cocaine use, other areas have more recently experienced the most rapid growth. Use of cocaine is showing potential signs of peaking in London and in the South of England, while continuing to rise in the North of England, for example.
- Cocaine use continued to be most prevalent in affluent urban areas (11%), but levels appeared to be harmonising outside these areas as well (at between 3 to 5%).
- Before 2000, cocaine use was more prevalent among the unemployed but, in 2000, its use was as common among those economically inactive or with a job. Use of hallucinogens (LSD and magic mushrooms) declined among the unemployed from peaks of up to 12 per cent in the mid-nineties to around one per cent in 2000.

Ethnic comparisons (Chapter 4)

As with the 1994 and 1996 sweeps, data from the 2000 survey included an ethnic booster sample to enable sufficiently sensitive analyses of the differences in drug use across ethnic groups. In addition to the main sample of 19,411, the booster included interviews with 3,874 respondents. The main findings were:

- Cannabis was the most common drug taken during people's lives, irrespective of ethnicity.
- Lifetime use of any drug among those aged 16 to 59 was greatest in the white group (34%), followed by 28 per cent of black people, 15 per cent of Indians and ten per cent of Pakistani/Bangladeshis.
- Among those respondents aged between 16 to 29 and 16 to 59, white people reported statistically significantly higher lifetime rates of cannabis, amphetamine, ecstasy, Class A drugs and 'any drug' use than other ethnic groups. Among 16- to 29-year-olds, lifetime use of Class A drugs and amphetamine among Indians equated to, or exceeded, that of black groups.
- Lifetime drug use among older respondents (30–59) was slightly higher among the white group (28% had tried a drug) in comparison to black groups. Asian drug use was around a third the level of white drug use. Lifetime drug use was higher in whites than blacks in all three age groups, and in the 30 to 59 group,

whites had the highest prevalence for amphetamine, Class A drugs and any drug compared to the other main ethnic groups.

- A closer examination of ethnic minority categories identified high lifetime prevalence among those of 'mixed ethnicity'.
- An examination of trends in lifetime use among the different ethnic groups showed no statistically significant changes in the use of heroin in any age group, although small increases were noted in the white and Indian groups. Significant increases in the lifetime prevalence rate for whites were noted for cannabis, cocaine, amphetamine and ecstasy. The proportions using crack, cocaine and ecstasy increased significantly in the Indian ethnic group.
- Among those aged 16 to 29, increased lifetime prevalence rates for any drug use among whites constituted the only statistically significant change from 1994. For those aged 16 to 59, a similar, significant increase in the lifetime use was noted among whites and Indians. Pakistani/Bangladeshi use significantly declined during this period. Last year use of any drug among respondents aged 16 to 29 increased significantly among Indians only.

Tracking the progress of the anti-drugs strategy (Chapter 5)

The Government's anti-drugs strategy aims to secure reductions in the proportion of young people using illegal drugs in the previous year and last month. A more specific goal, as discussed in the last BCS drugs report, is to reduce heroin and cocaine use by 25 per cent by 2005 and 50 per cent by 2008. More recently, this has been superseded by a broader target of reducing Class A drug use among the under 25s.

This chapter focuses on those aged 16 to 24, since this is the target age group for the Government's anti-drugs strategy. The main area of interest is how Class A drug use has changed since the 1998 baseline levels. It is important to look at heroin and cocaine use in particular, however, as these are considered the drugs that cause the greatest harm. It is also helpful to consider the broader and longer-term picture, and drug use by 16- to 24-year-olds across earlier sweeps of the BCS (since 1994) is presented.

Changes in drug use for the 16 to 24 age group from 1998 broadly mirror those for the wider 16 to 29 age group. The main findings for the 16 to 24s were:

- Use of any drug in the last year remained stable at 29 per cent for each of the four comparable sweeps of the BCS.

- Similarly, no significant change occurred for use of cannabis, with 26 per cent having used it within the last year.
- The proportion using cocaine rose significantly between 1994 and 2000 (from 1% to 5% for use in the last year and from less than 0.5% to 2% for use in the last month). Between 1998 and 2000, increases in cocaine use were not statistically significant.
- Use of heroin remained low, with no significant changes in last year or last month rates of use. Between 1998 and 2000, use in the last year rose from less than 0.5 per cent to one per cent; use in the last month remained at less than 0.5 per cent.
- Use of Class A drugs remained fairly stable between surveys, with use in the last year increasing slightly from eight per cent in 1998 to nine per cent in 2000; use in the last month increased from three per cent in 1998 to five per cent in 2000. Neither increase was statistically significant.

1 Introduction

Scope of the report

This report is the fourth in a series that presents comparable information about patterns of drug use in England and Wales. The British Crime Survey (BCS) included an almost identical drugs self-report component in each of four sweeps, carried out in 1994, 1996, 1998 and 2000. This report, like its predecessors, provides an assessment of continuity and change in the prevalence of prohibited drug use by the general population aged 16 to 59.

Regular surveys of drug use came into being in many European countries during the 1990s, typically with direct or indirect support from national governments (Bless *et al.*, 1997). Governments needed to take stock of a newly problematic set of behaviours by young people in particular; they also wanted to see whether their fledgling drugs strategies were having any impact. For England and Wales, the role of the BCS as a means of tracking changes in the prevalence of drug use was established informally with the first two comparable sweeps, in 1994 and 1996. The 1998 BCS has been formally recognised as constituting the baseline for the Government's long-term, anti-drugs strategy. For the 11 to 15 age group, a survey carried out in schools provides a complementary baseline. In the anti-drugs strategy, the first of four aims is "to help young people resist drug misuse in order to achieve their full potential in society" (UKADCU, 2000). Linked to this objective is a key performance target:

> To reduce the proportion of people under the age of 25 reporting the use of Class A drugs by 25% by 2005 and 50% by 2008.

The original target was to reduce heroin and cocaine use in under-25s by 25 per cent by 2005 and 50 per cent by 2008. However, this has since been superseded by the Class A target (UKADCU, 2001).

The specific Class A drugs covered by BCS questions are those most commonly used: heroin, cocaine (both powder and 'crack', the latter being a 'cooked' form of cocaine), ecstasy, magic mushrooms, LSD and unprescribed use of Methadone (a synthetic form of heroin). There are many other drugs also categorised as Class A in the often-amended second schedule of the Misuse of Drugs Act 1971, but they are in practice relatively obscure. While this report pays greater attention than its predecessors to patterns of use of the combined group of Class A drugs, it does still discuss prevalence rates both for individual drug types and for the use of any drug.

In line with the key performance target, this report concentrates on comparatively recent drug use (in the last year or month), rather than on drug use on a lifetime or 'ever' footing. In addition, the emphasis is largely but not exclusively on young people. That is particularly so in Chapter 5, which delivers the initial progress report on the anti-drugs strategy's key objective, and is concerned just with those under the age of 25. Elsewhere, other age groups are considered. For instance, with recent drug use peaking, typically, among those in their late teens, it is interesting to scrutinise prevalence rates for those aged 16 to 19, which can help us to anticipate future trends. And, while drug use tends to decrease for those in their 20s, the prevalence of cocaine use is highest among men aged 25 to 29. So, there is also some justification for continuing to look, as in previous reports, at young people in their late 20s, as well as those under 25.

The report is structured as follows:

This chapter provides a brief overview of the BCS as a drugs survey, its strengths and weaknesses, and its past and future development. Other relevant surveys are briefly discussed. There is also a succinct introduction to the drugs self-report component of the BCS, which respondents are asked to complete by means of laptop computers.

Chapter 2, entitled 'Current patterns of drug use', draws simply on the results of the 2000 BCS, particularly for young people aged 16 to 29. Prevalence rates are explored in terms of key factors, notably gender and age group; region and type of neighbourhood; income, educational level and social class; and lifestyle characteristics. The focus is partly on consumption of 'any drug'; also on specific drugs (notably cocaine) or groups of drugs (particularly those legally defined as Class A). Finally, estimates are provided of numbers of young people who had used various drugs in the last year.

Chapter 3, entitled 'Changing patterns of drug use, 1994 to 2000', assesses continuity and change in the prevalence of drug use across four sweeps of the BCS. The broad picture presented is of some stability in consumption levels for young people, male and female. The decline in the use of drugs in general, by the 16 to 19 age group, is discussed; so too is the increase in the prevalence of cocaine, across the 16 to 29 age group, particularly for men. The chapter also shows how a focus on regional variation, on employment status and on ACORN residential area classifications can help to shed light on the extent of change across England and Wales.

Chapter 4, entitled 'Ethnic comparisons', looks at drug use by different ethnic groups. Patterns of use by the various minority groups are presented, alongside those of their white counterparts. In addition, there is a review of minority ethnic drug use since the 1994 BCS. This was the first time that the existing drugs self-completion module was introduced, not only for the general population sample but also for an ethnic booster sample. The booster exercise was repeated in 1996 and 2000 (though not in 1998), enabling comparisons to be made. Minority ethnic respondents were also included in the main sample, as presented in the other chapters of this report; however, only in this chapter, which also draws on the booster sample, are results given specifically for minority ethnic groups.

Chapter 5, entitled 'Tracking the progress of the anti-drugs strategy', assesses initial efforts to reduce drug use by young people aged 16 to 24, since the 1998 baseline. The focus is mainly on Class A drugs in general and heroin and cocaine in particular, for the last year and month. Any change is extremely limited. So, by way of broader perspectives, the chapter also tracks these prevalence rates back to 1994, and provides estimates, for 2000, of the numbers of young people aged 16 to 24 who had used heroin, cocaine and Class A drugs in the last year and month.

The BCS as a survey of drug use

The BCS is a household survey, based on a representative, random sample across England and Wales, rather than on quotas. It is a well-established survey, enjoying a good response rate (for further details on sampling and response rates, see Appendix A). Within each household, one person is selected, also at random, to be interviewed about victimisation and other crime-related topics. All 13,300 respondents aged less than 60 were asked, at the end of the main interview, to self-complete the drugs component: 13,021 agreed (98%).

As a survey of households, the BCS does not cover some small groups, potentially important given that they may have relatively high rates of drug use: notably the homeless, and those living in certain institutions, such as prisons or student halls of residence. Nor, in practice, does any household survey necessarily reach people whose lives are so busy or chaotic that they are hardly ever at home. Lastly, household surveys usually have age criteria; in the BCS, from 1994 through to 2000, those aged under 16 were not eligible for interview, while those aged 60 or over were not asked to complete the drugs component (the decision to exclude the latter was an economy measure, reflecting their very low prevalence rates for the use of prohibited drugs). As previously mentioned, the anti-drugs strategy relies on a school-based survey, to cover those aged 11 to 15; this was first carried out in 1999, although questions on drugs were also included in another schools survey carried out in the previous year (Goddard and Higgins, 2000). It is worth noting that schools surveys, with their younger age group, have lower prevalence rates for Class A drugs than do household surveys such as the BCS, with their older respondents. Use of Class A drugs in the last year and last month were three per cent and one per cent respectively in the 1999 schools survey (the latest available for the 11 to 15 age group), as opposed to eight per cent and three per cent for those aged 16 to 24 in the 2000 BCS. Key findings, over time, from schools surveys are discussed in the next section.

In tracking changes in the level of drug use through the BCS, arguably what matters is that, irrespective of any strengths or weaknesses, it is a consistent instrument, deployed in the same fashion for each sweep. This was true both of the BCS in general for the period 1994 to 2000 and for the drugs component. In future, as discussed below, some changes are planned but, for these years, a high level of consistency was maintained. The new changes should not however be as dramatic as those differentiating the drugs components of the 1992 BCS (when a paper and pencil methodology was used) and the 1994 BCS (with self-completion by laptop computer); that particular change meant that it was difficult to make comparisons on drug use between those two sweeps of the BCS (Ramsay and Percy, 1997).

The role of the BCS specifically as a drugs survey continues to raise some important questions. The drugs component is, after all, no more than 'piggybacked' conveniently on a survey designed for another purpose. The arrangement has both pluses and minuses. There are three powerful advantages:

- the combination is cost-effective, since the marginal cost of the drugs component is very modest compared with a dedicated drugs survey
- as the BCS becomes an annual survey, from 2001, drug use can in future be tracked year in, year out
- with the BCS sample size roughly doubling from 2001, to around 40,000 respondents, it will be possible in future to track the prevalence of even the rarest drugs, such as heroin and crack, with enhanced precision.

There are also three drawbacks:

- The fact that the bulk of the questionnaire is already committed to questions about victimisation means that only a limited set of questions can be asked about drug use. There is no opportunity, for instance, to explore attitudes to drugs as well as drug-using behaviour (let alone the interaction of attitudes and behaviour); or to build up a more detailed social and psychological profile of respondents, whether users or non-users.

- It has always been recognised in BCS drugs reports, that the crime/victimisation context of the main interview is likely to influence the reporting of drug use. In other words, the prevalence rates presented in later chapters will tend to be underestimates.
- England and Wales share a criminal justice system, different from those of Scotland[1] and Northern Ireland, and thus it is unsurprising that each jurisdiction generally supports its own crime survey. This may help to explain why each of those surveys is currently carried out in different ways, with distinctive drugs components. The net result is a lack of full comparability across the UK.

For the time being, while the whole range of issues inherent in drugs surveys remains under review, the BCS will remain the main vehicle for estimating the prevalence of drug use in England and Wales.

One further modification to the BCS for 2001 onwards is the addition, for those aged 16 to 24, of some questions about access to drugs and age of first use, and the deletion of the existing questions about awareness of different drugs. These additions should not influence trends as they are placed at the end of the module. For the 2000 BCS, however, the drugs component remains, for the last time, almost entirely unchanged, so that comparability with the three previous sweeps of the BCS is extremely good. The current set of BCS drugs questions is discussed in the final section of this chapter; they are also reproduced in Appendix F.

Other surveys of drug use

The BCS has no monopoly in the field of drugs surveys. Other surveys help to provide a fuller picture of patterns of drug use in England and Wales, particularly in terms of the important issue of change over time. A few of these surveys are discussed here, briefly. In recent years, the only major surveys of drug use by the adult population are the two sweeps of the National Drugs Campaign Survey (NDCS) in England in 1995 and 1996 (McNeill and Raw, 1997; Tasker et al., 1999) and the 1998/9 Youth Lifestyles Survey (YLS) in England and Wales, which followed an earlier sweep in 1992/3 (Graham and Bowling, 1995; Flood-Page et al., 2000). Because of a change in sampling methods, coupled with a

---

1 The Scottish survey is still entirely conducted on paper and may reduce disclosure on the self-completion elements of the survey.

relatively short interval in between the two fieldwork phases, the results of the two NDCS sweeps do not offer any authoritative assessment of change over time. Equally, because the two sweeps of the YLS involved different self-report methodologies (a tick-box form in 1992/3 as opposed to a laptop module in 1998/9), their results are not sufficiently comparable to track changes in the prevalence of drug use. However, these surveys do provide fresh insights into patterns of drug use, including drug use by vulnerable groups such as truants or runaways (Goulden and Sondhi, 2001). Also, they tend broadly to confirm the BCS prevalence levels, even if there are elements of divergence (Ramsay and Percy, 1997).

Various schools surveys provide clearer insights into prevalence changes over time. First, two sets of surveys provide a reasonably long view across a number of years. As part of a European research project, Martin Plant and Patrick Miller of the Edinburgh-based Alcohol and Health Research Centre carried out surveys of pupils aged around 15 or 16, throughout the UK, in both 1995 and 1999. They reported a decrease in the use of most types of drugs, except heroin and cocaine (Miller and Plant, 1996; Miller and Plant, 2000). Their sample was a systematic one (from randomly selected schools), although numbers dropped substantially between the two sweeps, from 7,700 in 1995 to 2,600 in 1999.

John Balding, of the Exeter-based Schools Health Education Unit, regularly facilitates a schools survey, which began in the 1980s. Very large numbers of pupils take part each year, across the UK, primarily in England and Scotland, although there is no consistent sampling of particular schools. Results from this series also point to decreases in drug use among 14- to 15-year-olds in the late 1990s, starting in 1997 (Balding, 2000).

Second, in addition to these two non-governmental surveys, the Department of Health commissions school-based surveys to complement the BCS in monitoring the progress of the anti-drugs strategy. The Department has sponsored a biennial survey of smoking and/or drinking by 11- to 15-year-olds in England since 1982, first adding some questions on drug use in 1998 – a formula also followed in 2000. In 1999, a slightly different schools survey was carried out, concentrating on illicit drug use, but also covering the 'legal' drugs; this is being repeated in 2001. With results now available for 1998 and 1999, the emerging picture from this sequence of representative samples is of stability over time in prevalence levels, if anything with slight increases rather than decreases (Goddard and Higgins, 2000). However, this series of schools-based drugs surveys covers a more limited period than the others previously discussed, but does provide a representative random sample of school children.

In conclusion, there is no clear-cut message to emerge from these other surveys of drug use, most of them carried out in schools. There are some indications of reductions in use in the late 1990s (Balding, 2000; Milller and Plant, 2000); on the other hand, surveys sponsored by the Department of Health point if anything to modest increases in prevalence, admittedly only for a rather short, recent period of time, from 1998 (Goddard and Higgins, 2000). None of these different surveys demonstrate any substantial growth in levels of drug use.

The drugs self-report component of the BCS

Respondents self-completed the BCS drugs component by means of laptop computers. The laptop was handed to them by the interviewer, at the close of a traditional face-to-face interview, chiefly about experiences of crime or victimisation. When respondents had finished the self-report component, their answers were electronically scrambled, and they were then able to pass the laptop back to the interviewer. As discussed in previous BCS reports, the use of laptops rather than paper self-completion forms seems to have worked well and even to have empowered respondents to some degree. The National Household Survey on Drug Abuse, the most important survey of its kind in the US, also currently employs laptops for self-reporting of drug use (SAMHSA, 2000), as does the Northern Ireland Crime Survey (Hague et al., 2000).

The whole self-report process in the 2000 BCS was a straightforward one, with only six per cent of the 13,021 respondents aged 16 to 59 having to be helped out by the interviewer (see Appendix A for further details). Participants worked their way through a sequence of on-screen questions, selecting 'yes', 'no', 'don't know' or 'don't want to answer' options, by keying in one of various numbers. The first sequence of questions about drug use concerned respondents' lifetime experience ('ever') of 17 specified substances. Those respondents who answered 'yes' for any of these drug types were then asked whether or not they had taken them in the last year; while finally those who had used any drug in the last year were asked whether or not they had taken them in the last month. It is perhaps worth adding that the 'last year', for the purposes of the 2000 BCS, for which, as usual, fieldwork was carried out mainly in the first quarter or soon afterwards, meant a period of twelve months prior to interview, stretching back substantially into 1999.

The list of drug types, about which respondents were asked, and for which they were given street names, comprised:

- amphetamine
- cannabis

- cocaine
- crack
- ecstasy
- heroin
- LSD
- magic mushrooms
- Methadone, not prescribed by a doctor
- Semeron (a bogus drug, discussed below)
- tranquillisers such as Valium or Temazepam, unprescribed
- amyl nitrite/poppers
- steroids, unprescribed
- glue, solvents, gas or aerosols
- pills or powders, unknown
- smoked something other than tobacco, unknown
- anything else considered to be a drug, unprescribed.

By way of 'warm-up' before tackling those questions about drug use, and to assess levels of awareness, respondents were asked first whether they had heard of the initial 13 substances – those of a relatively specific nature. As shown in Appendix B (Table B.1), a very high proportion of respondents recognised each of the different drug types. Leaving aside Semeron, the bogus drug, over 90 per cent of all those aged 16 to 59 reported that they had heard of nearly all the 13 drugs. The three substances commanding the lowest levels of awareness were magic mushrooms (89%), Methadone (87%) and amyl nitrite/poppers (70%). These were still relatively large majorities, and they were all significantly higher than equivalent figures in 1994 (when they were 80%, 66% and 63% respectively). The largest increase in awareness was for Methadone, a synthetic form of heroin, which has an important, legitimate role in treatment but also leaks into a 'black market'.

Given a society with so developed a level of drugs awareness, the fact that five per cent of all respondents reported that they had heard of Semeron, a bogus substance, raises as many questions as it answers. Semeron sounds relatively plausible, so perhaps some respondents were 'confused'. Hardly any of those respondents reporting their awareness of Semeron subsequently declared they had used it: just three people said they had ever done so, and one did so for the last year (there were no last month reports of Semeron use). There is arguably a case for no longer 'misleading' the public with Semeron, now that the validity of household surveys has broadly been established. In the next BCS (2001), the initial sequence of 13 questions on awareness of different substances, real and bogus, has been abolished (to compensate for this, respondents can select a 'Never heard of it' response to 'ever taken' questions). The awareness questions are no longer seen as a worthwhile use of interview time. Even in the 2000 BCS, the most important questions are those directly addressing drug use, with which the rest of this report is concerned.

Current patterns of drug use

Introduction

This chapter focuses on current drug use patterns among the general population of England and Wales. It opens by outlining some basic features of the prevalence of different types of drug use, particularly in terms of age and gender and there follows an analysis of the geographical and socio-economic dimensions of drug use. The most relevant factors, as highlighted in earlier BCS drugs reports, are:

- variation by region and by type of neighbourhood
- variation in terms of income, educational level and social class
- variation in terms of lifestyle characteristics such as social and leisure activities.

While BCS respondents were asked about their drug use over three different timescales – 'lifetime', 'in the last year' and 'in the last month' – this chapter places its main emphasis on use in the last year. This is a reasonable indicator of relatively recent drug use and more often provides a larger sample of users that enables statistical comparisons between groups to be more robust (see Appendix E for further details of the statistical tests used in this report). Nevertheless, some attention is also paid to lifetime and last-month drug use, where these are thought to be important.

Most of this chapter focuses on younger people, aged 16 to 29, as this age group tends to have higher rates of drug use than do older people. The 16 to 24 age group will also be considered independently, as those under 25 constitute the population targeted by the Government's anti-drugs strategy. Chapter 5 deals with drug use among this target group of young people. Baseline figures for this group were established by the 1998 British Crime Survey, and targets were set for reducing their use of drugs (particularly Class A drugs) by 2005 and 2008 (by 25% and 50% respectively).

Other reasons for considering the wider age range are that, although there is a tendency for those approaching 30 to desist from drug use, there are at least some types of drug for which those in their later 20s have rates as high, or higher, than younger people do. Additionally, there were almost twice as many respondents sampled in the wider, 16 to 29 age range (3,015) compared with 16- to 24-year-olds (1,517) in the 2000 BCS. This allows for slightly more detailed breakdowns according to characteristics such as region or ACORN category and increases the sensitivity of statistical testing of differences between groups.

The main drug groups mentioned in previous surveys have been 'hallucinants' (amphetamine, LSD, magic mushrooms, ecstasy and poppers) and 'opiates+' (heroin, Methadone, cocaine, and crack). These categories made particularly good sense at the point when they were first used, in the report on the 1994 BCS, although the increasing importance of cocaine in more recent years presents a complicating factor. Analysis has shown that use of opiates+ drugs has increasingly been driven by consumption of cocaine. Use of the other three drugs in this category (Methadone, heroin and crack) has remained considerably less widespread. Therefore, it has become more appropriate to examine cocaine and heroin separately. Some data for the opiates+ group are, however, included, especially in tables in Appendix B.

While hallucinants were widely used in the context of the rave or dance scene of the early to mid 1990s, fashions have changed since then, as noted in the last two BCS drugs reports. In particular, cocaine has grown in popularity alongside the hallucinants, in club/dance settings since the late 1990s. So, there is also less value in continuing to focus on the hallucinants group of drugs.

Age and gender

The results of the BCS showed that drug use was more prevalent in younger people. The lifetime, last year and last month prevalence rates for use of any drug (i.e. any of the 17 drug types listed in the previous chapter and as shown in Tables B.2 to B.5 in Appendix B) were highest in the 20 to 24 age group, at 58 per cent, 30 per cent and 20 per cent respectively. Table 2.1 below shows that 25 per cent of all 16- to 29-year-olds reported using drugs in the last year. An interesting point in Table 2.1 is that 50 per cent of 16 to 29s had tried prohibited drugs at some point in their lives. However, we cannot conclude from this that drug use is becoming 'normalised' (i.e. the process of being accepted as a normal, or more correctly normative, behaviour by the general public or certain sub-groups), given that lifetime usage rates were much higher than those for periods that were more recent. A more in-depth discussion of issues around normalisation of drug use can be found in Parker et al. (1998) and Shiner and Newburn (1997 & 1998).

Men were more likely to report the use of drugs than women were. For the whole sample (16 to 59s), the proportions of men and women having ever used drugs were 40 per cent and 28 per cent respectively (a male/female ratio of 1.4:1). This gap widens progressively with equivalent ratios for the last year (1.8:1) and the last month (2.3:1). The ratios of male to female drug use were all lower for the younger age groups. However, there was a similar widening of the gender gap for more recent drug use in contrast with lifetime experience. This indicates that, in very general terms, women are more experimental in their drug use and mature out of it sooner than men do.

Table 2.1: *Percentage of respondents using drugs in their lifetime, the last year and the last month by age group and sex*

	16–19	20–24	25–29	16–29	30–59	16–59
Lifetime						
Men	44	63	60	56	34	40
Women	40	54	40	44	22	28
All	42	58	50	50	28	34
Ratio men/women	1.1	1.2	1.5	1.3	1.5	1.4
Last year						
Men	31	34	26	30	8	14
Women	24	26	14	20	4	8
All	27	30	20	25	5	11
Ratio men/women	1.3	1.3	1.9	1.5	2.0	1.8
Last month						
Men	21	23	19	21	4	9
Women	12	16	6	11	2	4
All	16	20	12	16	3	6
Ratio men/women	1.8	1.4	3.2	1.9	2.0	2.3

Note: Sample sizes for this table and all the others in this chapter can be found in Appendix A. Source: 2000 BCS (weighted data).

Number of drugs used

Most young people tended to restrict their use to a single drug, with 15 per cent of 16 to 29s having used just one drug type, possibly on various occasions, in the last year; ten per cent had taken upwards of two different drugs. Cannabis was usually the drug taken by single drug users. Of the group of users taking three or more drugs in the last year, the most commonly used were: cannabis (95%), ecstasy (69%), amphetamine (62%) and cocaine (57%).

Table 2.2: Percentage of respondents aged 16 to 29 using varying numbers of drugs

	No drugs	One drug	Two drugs	Three or more
Use in the last year	75	15	4	6
Use in the last month	84	11	3	2

Source: 2000 BCS (weighted data).

Different drugs

Only certain drugs and groups of drugs will be discussed in this section, although tables detailing use of all the various drugs on a lifetime basis, in the last year and in the last month among different age groups can be found in Appendix B (Tables B.2 to B.5).

Cannabis

Of all the various drugs, cannabis was the most commonly used, with 27 per cent of respondents aged 16 to 59 having tried it within their lifetime, nine per cent having used it in the last year and six per cent in the last month. Its use was highest among the younger age groups, with use among 16- to 29-year-olds in their lifetime, the last year and the last month at 44, 22 and 14 per cent respectively. Rates of use were higher in men across all age groups.

Amphetamine

After cannabis, amphetamine was the most commonly used drug, with 22 per cent of 16- to 29-year-olds having taken it in their lifetime; five per cent having used it in the last year and two per cent in the last month. The highest use was seen in 16- to 19-year-old men, where eight per cent had used in the last year and five per cent in the last month.

Hallucinants

As previously mentioned, this group of drugs consists of amphetamine, LSD, magic mushrooms, ecstasy and poppers, all of which have been associated with the dance scene. A considerable proportion (29%) of young people aged 16 to 29 had tried hallucinants in their lifetime. Use of these drugs within the last year and the last month was much lower at nine per cent and five per cent respectively. The highest rates for use in the last year and last month were in the 20 to 24 age group (11% and 6%).

Table 2.3: *Percentage of respondents using hallucinants in their lifetime, the last year and the last month by age group*

	16–19	20–24	25–29	16–29	30–59	16–59
Lifetime	19	36	31	29	12	16
Last year	9	11	8	9	1	3
Last month	5	6	4	5	-	2

Note: '-' indicates less than 0.5% (this convention is used in the rest of the tables in this chapter). Source: 2000 BCS (weighted data).

Opiates+

This group of drugs is associated with more problematic use, due to their highly addictive nature, and comprises heroin, cocaine, crack and Methadone. Crack is a 'cooked' form of cocaine, while Methadone is a synthetic equivalent of heroin, widely used in the treatment of drug-dependent people, but sometimes also taken for non-medical purposes. The highest rates for use of these drugs within the last year were found in those in their early to mid 20s (7%). However, the 16 to 19 age group had the highest rate for use in the last month (3%). As previously noted in the introduction to this chapter, cocaine was by far the most widely used of this set of drugs.

Table 2.4: *Percentage of respondents using opiates+ in their lifetime, the last year and the last month by age group*

	16–19	20–24	25–29	16–29	30–59	16–59
Lifetime	7	14	11	11	3	5
Last year	4	7	5	5	1	2
Last month	3	2	2	2	-	1

Source: 2000 BCS (weighted data).

The different levels of use for heroin, Methadone and crack were all very low indeed. Among 16- to 29-year-olds, the rate for use within the last year was around one per cent for heroin and crack and slightly lower for Methadone. Although the data obtained from this survey indicate that use of these drugs is low, the prevalence in groups such as homeless people, who are not reachable through household surveys, may be higher (Wade and Barnett, 1999).

Cocaine

Table 2.5 shows that the prevalence of cocaine use is higher in younger people, with five per cent of the 16- to 29-year-olds having used it within the last year. Compared with cannabis, or general patterns of drug use, cocaine is proportionally more prevalent among men than women; it is more expensive than other drugs (Corkery, 2001), is often consumed alongside copious quantities of alcohol (Pearson, 1998), and is perhaps a drug for 'affluent lads'. Men generally have higher incomes than women do (The Women's Unit, 2001[2]) and their consumption of alcohol is higher (Department of Health, 1999[3]), which may explain some of the gender difference. Among 16- to 29-year-olds, cocaine is now almost as popular as ecstasy in terms of use within the last year; in some parts of the country, as discussed later in this chapter, cocaine is in fact more widespread. One possible explanation for this is that cocaine is considered by some young users to be more socially acceptable than other stimulants and not as dangerous (Boys et al., 2001).

Cocaine use has mostly been associated with those in their 20s and this survey found that the highest prevalence for use in the last year was for males in their 20s (8%). However, the rate for the male 16 to 19 age group was not far behind, at six per cent. Indeed, no significant difference was found in the rates across the three youngest age groups (16–19, 20–24 and 25–29) and it has been suggested elsewhere that patterns of cocaine use are changing, becoming less exceptional among younger groups (Boys et al., 2001).

Table 2.5: *Percentage of respondents using cocaine in their lifetime, the last year and the last month by age group and sex*

	16–19	20–24	25–29	16–29	30–59	16–59
Lifetime						
Men	8	16	17	14	4	7
Women	4	11	5	7	2	3
All	6	14	11	10	3	5
Last year						
Men	6	8	8	7	1	3
Women	2	4	2	3	-	1
All	4	6	5	5	1	2
Last month						
Men	3	2	4	3	-	1
Women	1	-	-	1	-	-
All	2	1	2	2	-	1

Source: 2000 BCS (weighted data).

2 See website at www.womens-unit.gov.uk
3 See website at www.doh.gov.uk/public/sb9924.htm

Class A drugs

This group of drugs is in legal terms ranked as the most serious, and penalties for use or possession tend to be higher (Misuse of Drugs Act, 1971). The Class A drugs covered in the BCS are those most widely used: cocaine, crack, ecstasy, heroin, LSD, magic mushrooms and Methadone. Of these, cocaine and ecstasy are more widely used than the rest.

Table 2.6 shows that just over a fifth of young people aged 16 to 29 had used Class A drugs in their lifetime; the proportion consuming these drugs in the last year and last month was considerably lower. The highest rate of use within the last year was seen in the 20 to 24 age group (10%).

Table 2.6: Percentage of respondents using Class A drugs in their lifetime, the last year and the last month by age group

	16–19	20–24	25–29	16–29	30–59	16–59
Lifetime	14	27	22	21	8	11
Last year	8	10	6	8	1	3
Last month	5	5	3	4	-	1

Source: 2000 BCS (weighted data).

Regional variations

Figure 2.1 shows that use of any drug in the last year by 16- to 29-year-olds was highest in London (31%), Anglia (28%) and the North (26%). Rates in London were significantly higher compared with the Midlands and Wales ($p<0.05$). Use of Class A drugs in the last year among this age group was significantly higher in London (13%) compared with the South ($p<0.05$), Wales ($p<0.01$) and the Midlands ($p<0.01$). A more detailed breakdown of drug use split by the ten Government Office Regions is found in Table B.6 in Appendix B. This also shows that London has consistently higher rates of any drug and Class A use.

Figure 2.1: **Percentage of respondents aged 16 to 29 using any drug and Class A drugs in the last year**

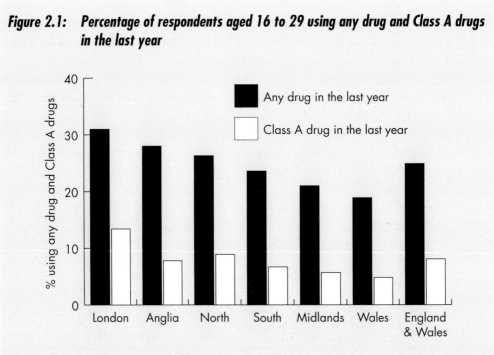

Note: These six regions are a condensed set of the nine standard English and Welsh regions, assembled as follows: London = Greater London; Anglia = East Anglia; North = North + Yorkshire & Humberside + North West; South = South East + South West; Midlands = East Midlands + West Midlands; Wales = Wales. Source: 2000 BCS (weighted data).

Drug use is not spread evenly around the country and prevalence rates for particular drugs vary considerably by region. There are a number of possible reasons for this regional disparity. For instance, there are considerable variations in regional levels of alcohol consumption and smoking (Department of Health, 1996[4]). These variations may well be associated with different levels of use of prohibited drugs; research has found strong links between alcohol and drug use (Leitner et al., 1993). Another point, also discussed in previous BCS reports (Ramsay and Partridge, 1999), is that the diffusion of new types of drug often starts in London and then spreads to other regions; also, London consistently tends to have the highest rates of use.

Figure 2.2 illustrates the pattern of cocaine use in 16- to 29-year-olds across regions. For use in the last year, London was found to have significantly higher rates than the South, the North, Wales and the Midlands (p<0.01). London does not stand out so much for last month cocaine use, which seems more evenly spread across the regions. Although these patterns

4 See website at www.official-documents/doh/survey96/ehch8.htm

may illustrate the diffusion of cocaine use to other regions, the low sample sizes (especially for Anglia) should be taken into consideration. Cocaine use in the ten Government Office Regions is reported in Table B.6 in Appendix B for the 16 to 29 age group.

Figure 2.2: **Percentage of respondents aged 16 to 29 using cocaine in the last year and last month by region**

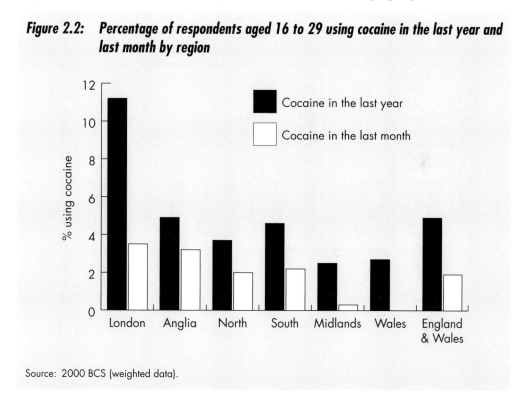

Source: 2000 BCS (weighted data).

Figure 2.3 shows heroin, cocaine and ecstasy use in the last year among 16- to 29-year-olds. Use of heroin was highest in the North (1%), the Midlands (1%) and the South (1%). Ecstasy use was highest in London (7%), closely followed by the North (6%). The chart indicates that, in some areas (namely, London, the South and Wales), the proportion of young people using cocaine was higher than that for ecstasy. It has been suggested that some young people may be substituting cocaine for other stimulants such as ecstasy – one possible reason being that the effects of using cocaine are perceived to be easier to manage (Boys *et al.*, 2001). In addition, much of the media attention on drugs seems to focus on the harms related to ecstasy use, which may have inadvertently assisted in making cocaine a more attractive choice to young people.

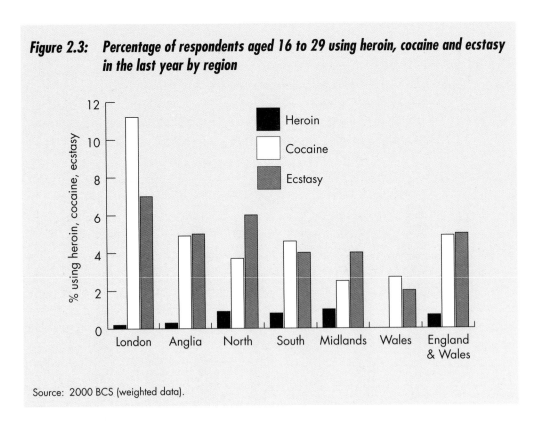

Figure 2.3: *Percentage of respondents aged 16 to 29 using heroin, cocaine and ecstasy in the last year by region*

Source: 2000 BCS (weighted data).

Socio-economic factors

A combination of many different factors may influence whether an individual will use drugs – the type of neighbourhood lived in, income level, educational attainment and lifestyle are some examples. One common assumption, for example, is that more problematic forms of drug use are linked to socio-economic deprivation (ACMD, 1998). In order to examine possible relationships, cross-tabulations of drug use with a range of socio-economic variables were carried out.

ACORN category

This classifies a household according to the demographic, employment and housing characteristics of its surrounding neighbourhood (CACI, 1993). It is based on analysis of the common socio-demographic features of different wards from 1991 census data. The categories can be defined as follows:
- A Affluent suburban and rural areas – 'Thriving'
- B Affluent family areas – 'Expanding'

- C Affluent urban areas – 'Rising'
- D Mature home-owning areas – 'Settling'
- E New home-owning areas – 'Aspiring'
- F Council estates and low-income areas – 'Striving'.

There was considerable variation in terms of drug use across the different ACORN categories. Table B.7 in Appendix B details use of any drug in the last year for the whole sample (16- to 59-year-olds), and shows that drug use ranged from seven per cent in affluent suburban/rural areas to 25 per cent in affluent urban areas. Although the latter are inhabited by a fairly well-off population, there is in fact quite a range of incomes. These areas also have a high proportion of young people – 40 per cent were aged 16 to 29 as opposed to only 18 per cent in affluent suburban/rural areas. This may help account for the considerably higher prevalence rate of drug use found. When focusing on the 16 to 29 age group only (see Figure 2.4 below), use of any drug in the last year was still significantly higher in the affluent urban areas compared with all the other groups (p<0.01). Similarly, use of any drug in the last month was significantly higher (p<0.05) in relation to all other ACORN areas, with the exception of council estates/low income areas.

Figure 2.4: **Percentage of respondents aged 16 to 29 using any drug in the last year and last month by ACORN category**

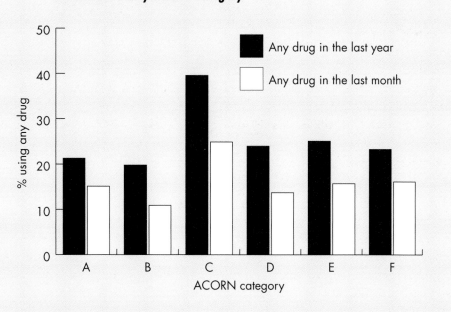

Note: A = Affluent suburban and rural areas; B = Affluent family areas; C = Affluent urban areas; D = Mature home-owning areas; E = New home-owning areas; F = Council estates and low-income areas. Source: 2000 BCS (weighted data).

Rates of use by 16- to 29-year-olds in the last year for hallucinants, cocaine and Class A drugs were likewise highest in affluent urban areas (see Table B.8 in Appendix B). However, there was a different pattern for the use of heroin and crack, which were less prevalent in these areas than elsewhere. Use of these drugs was more prevalent in mature and new home-owning and council estates/low income areas. Figure 2.5 illustrates how cocaine, heroin and Class A use varied across the different ACORN areas. No significant differences in rates for use of heroin were found, although these were generally higher in less affluent areas. For cocaine use, a significantly higher rate was found in those 16- to 29-year-olds living in affluent urban areas compared with affluent suburban/rural areas and new home-owning areas ($p<0.05$) and affluent family areas, mature home-owning areas and council estates/low-income areas ($p<0.01$). Similarly, for Class A drug use, a significantly higher rate was found in the affluent urban areas compared with affluent suburban/rural areas, affluent family areas and mature home-owning areas ($p<0.01$) and new home-owning areas and council estates/low income areas ($p<0.05$). When the 30 to 59 age group is examined, affluent urban areas again had the highest prevalence rates for use of any drug (see Table B.7 in Appendix B).

Figure 2.5: **Percentage of respondents aged 16 to 29 using heroin, cocaine and Class A drugs in the last year by ACORN category**

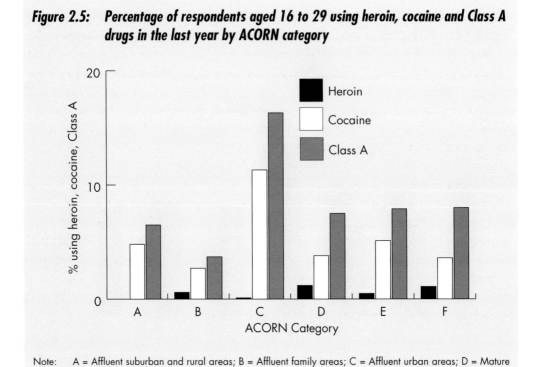

Note: A = Affluent suburban and rural areas; B = Affluent family areas; C = Affluent urban areas; D = Mature home-owning areas; E = New home-owning areas; F = Council estates and low-income areas. Source: 2000 BCS (weighted data).

Income, educational attainment, social class and employment status

These indicators can be used to help measure affluence in the general population and all are obviously inter-related. Tables 2.7, 2.8 and 2.9 below show how drug use in the last year varied by household income, education and social class. They highlight the point that different types of drug have very different relationships with socio-economic factors.

As shown in previous BCS drugs reports, Table 2.7 has a 'U-shaped' distribution between the three income groups, whereby the highest levels of drug use tend to be at the two extremes of the household income scale, and the lowest prevalence is in the middle-income groups. Because age might play a part in determining income level, the age distribution within each category was examined and this showed similar proportions of 16 to 19s, 20 to 24s and 25 to 29s in each. Cocaine use among those in the 'richest' income category was significantly higher than for the 'intermediate' category (7% compared with 4%; $p<0.05$). This is not surprising as cocaine has been linked with wealth, fashion and a glamorous lifestyle, described in one study as 'rich man's speed' – speed being a slang name for amphetamine (Boys *et al.*, 2001).

However, a similar level of use was found in the lowest income category (6%), which suggests that cocaine is not just a drug for the most affluent. Possible explanations for this include declining cocaine prices (Corkery, 2000), and the fact that it is becoming more popular with a younger age group, as discussed earlier in this chapter. Heroin use, on the other hand, does not fit into this pattern. The proportion who used heroin in the last year was found to be higher in the poorest households (3% compared with 0.5% in the intermediate group and less than 0.5% in the richest group; this was significantly higher in relation to the intermediate group only at $p<0.05$[5]).

Do drug use patterns vary among different educational groups? A survey of drug use among school children aged 11 to 15 (Goddard and Higgins, 2000) found that those who did not think they were going to live up to other people's expectations of them in terms of examination results had the highest levels of drug use. Table 2.8 shows educational attainment and drug use in the last year among three different age groups. Only data for 'no qualifications' and 'intermediate' qualifications are presented for the youngest age group as it is unlikely that any 16- to 19-year-old will have completed a degree (only 3 respondents in this age group said they had degree level qualifications or higher).

---

5 The number of respondents in the richest group is too small to allow the detection of any statistical difference between other income groups.

A similar pattern to income is displayed, whereby the intermediate group had a generally lower level of use for many drugs across all three age groups. Although no significant differences were found, a higher proportion of 16- to 19-year-olds without qualifications reported using any drug, Class A, cocaine and hallucinants compared to those who had intermediate level qualifications. The rate of use of cocaine in the last year was found to be higher (although not significantly) in those with degree level qualifications for the two older age groups. In contrast, none of those holding degree level qualifications reported using heroin in the last year. Use of heroin was more prevalent in those with fewer qualifications, which, given the link between qualifications and income, confirms the patterns of heroin use across income groups discussed previously.

Table 2.9, on social class, shows a contrast between cocaine and heroin use. Respondents in the 'top two' social class categories (consisting of 'professional' and 'managerial and technical' occupations) had a higher level of cocaine use in the last year (8% compared with 4% in the other groups). The difference between the 'intermediate' and 'top two' group was found to be statistically significant ($p<0.05$). Heroin use, on the other hand, was higher in the 'lowest' and 'intermediate' groups (although this was not found to be significantly higher). This reinforces the point that different types of drugs have different relationships with socio-economic factors.

Table 2.7: *Percentage of respondents aged 16 to 29 using various drugs in the last year by household income*

	Cocaine	Heroin	Hallucinants	Any drug	Class A
Poorest (<£5,000)	6	3	13	28	11
Intermediate (£5,000–£29,999)	4	-	8	25	6
Richest (£30,000+)	7	-	10	25	10

Source: 2000 BCS (weighted data).

Table 2.8: *Percentage of respondents using various drugs in the last year by age group and educational attainment*

	Cocaine	Heroin	Hallucinants	Any drug	Class A
16–19					
No qualifications	5	1	14	30	13
Intermediate	3	1	8	26	7
20–24					
No qualifications	8	3	12	43	15
Intermediate	5	1	11	27	9
Degree/higher degree	10	0	9	36	12
25–29					
No qualifications	5	2	6	17	6
Intermediate	4	-	7	19	6
Degree/higher degree	7	0	10	22	9

Note: Educational attainment groupings are defined as: No qualifications = no qualifications achieved; Intermediate = diplomas in higher education and other higher education certificates, A level or equivalent, O level or equivalent passes, O level or equivalent (grades D to F); Degree/higher degree = all degree level qualifications. Source: 2000 BCS (weighted data).

Table 2.9: *Percentage of respondents aged 16 to 29 using various drugs in the last year by social class*

	Cocaine	Heroin	Hallucinants	Any drug	Class A
Lowest	4	1	10	24	7
Intermediate	4	1	10	27	9
Top two	8	-	9	26	9

Note   Social class groupings are defined as: Lowest = unskilled occupations; Intermediate = skilled occupations (manual and non-manual) + partly skilled occupations; Top two = professional + managerial and technical occupations. Source: 2000 BCS (weighted data).

Employment status may also be linked to drug use, as shown in Table 2.10. Use within the last year of any drug, heroin and Class A drugs by 16- to 29-year-olds was higher among the unemployed. Table 2.10 shows that different patterns emerge for cocaine use in the last year, where the highest prevalence was found in those who were working. Although no significant differences in the rates of drug use between the three employment categories were found for the different types of drugs listed, the low rate for heroin use among those who were working is notable.

A report looking at environmental factors and drug misuse found that any statistical relationship between drug use and deprivation seemed to apply more to problematic drug use (ACMD, 1998). The results from the 2000 BCS are consistent with such findings, which suggest that cocaine use is relatively widespread across the general population, while heroin tends to be associated with less affluent groups. There may also be subtle biases in reported use of such a stigmatised drug as heroin among different social groupings.

Table 2.10: *Percentage of respondents aged 16 to 29 using various drugs in the last year by employment status*

	Cocaine	Heroin	Any drug	Class A
Employed	5	-	25	8
Unemployed	4	3	33	12
Economically inactive	4	1	22	8

Note: 'Employed' includes: people doing full-time or part-time paid work in the last week; working on a government supported training scheme; or doing unpaid work for own/family business. 'Economically inactive' includes: respondents of working age who are retired; going to school or college full-time; looking after home/family; are temporarily or permanently sick; or doing something else. 'Unemployed' includes those: actively seeking work, or waiting to take up work. Source: 2000 BCS (weighted data).

Other factors

Many other socio-economic factors could be used to examine drug use within the population. Housing tenure, for example, shows that owner-occupiers tended to have lower levels of use of any drug in the last year compared with those living in rented accommodation (see Table B.9 in Appendix B). A significantly higher prevalence of use in the last year was found for 16 to 29s in the private rented sector (33% compared with 23% for social rented housing and 19% for owned/part-owned; $p<0.01$). The older age group (30–59s) showed a similar pattern, with those who lived in the private rented sector having a significantly higher prevalence of drug use in the last year than those who owned their homes ($p<0.01$).

Drug use was also more prevalent in single people. Table B.10 in Appendix B shows that for both the 16–29 and 30–59 age groups, rates of use were highest in the single or separated/divorced groups. For those aged 16–29, a significantly higher ($p<0.01$) proportion (28%) of single respondents used drugs in the last year compared with married/cohabiting respondents (11%). This pattern was also seen in the older age group of 30 to 59s, where 13 per cent of single respondents compared with three per cent of married/cohabiting respondents used drugs in the last year ($p<0.01$).

Factors such as housing tenure and marital status combine 'socio-economic' and 'lifestyle' elements, of which both are among the many influences bearing on drug use. For instance, single people living in privately-rented bedsits may be more likely to go out in the evening, all of which are associated with use of drugs – it is vital to consider the role of lifestyle alongside socio-economic factors.

Lifestyle factors

Lifestyle may have a considerable influence on patterns of drug use. Table 2.11 shows that those visiting a pub or bar three or more times a week were about twice as likely to have used any drug in the last year. Frequent pub goers were more than three times as likely to have taken cocaine in the last year. Indeed, young cocaine users have reported a preference for visiting pubs and bars when taking cocaine, as the long queues in club toilets made it difficult for them to take the drug when they were out (Boys et al., 2001).

Table 2.12 shows that drug use in the last year also increased with the frequency of alcohol consumption. A significantly higher proportion of the most frequent drinkers aged 16 to 29 (40% compared with 24% in the intermediate group and 15% in the least frequent group; $p<0.01$) used drugs in the last year. Indeed, significantly higher rates among frequent drinkers were found for all the drugs listed in the table. The link between alcohol and drug use has also been highlighted in younger age groups (Goddard and Higgins, 2000), where 30 per cent of those who drank at least once a week had used drugs in the last month, compared with less than one per cent of those who had never had a drink. Research has highlighted that alcohol is often used in conjunction with certain drugs in order to help manage negative psychological effects. Cocaine users, for example, have reported how they used alcohol to help them cope with the paranoia and insomnia experienced after using cocaine (Boys et al., 2001).

Some types of drug use are specifically associated with the clubbing or dance culture (Parker et al., 1998). Table 2.13 shows that the likelihood of having used drugs within the last year was higher for those who attended night clubs more frequently. A significantly higher proportion of those who went clubbing at least once a week (39%) used any drug in the last year compared with those who went less than once a week (22%). Significantly higher rates for ecstasy, hallucinants and Class A drugs were also found in the more frequent clubbers. Although cocaine use was higher in the more frequent clubbers, the difference was not significant.

Table 2.11: Percentage of respondents aged 16 to 29 using various drugs in the last year by frequency of visits to the pub in the evening

	Cocaine	Ecstasy	Any drug	Hallucinants	Class A
Less than 3 times a week	3	4	20	7	6
3 or more times a week	**11	**9	**42	**16	**16

Note: **=significant difference between the two groups at $p<0.01$. Source: 2000 BCS (weighted data).

Table 2.12: Percentage of respondents aged 16 to 29 using various drugs in the last year by frequency of alcohol consumption

	Cocaine	Ecstasy	Any drug	Hallucinants	Class A
Drinks 3 or more days a week	10	10	40	16	16
Drinks 1 to 2 days a week	4	5	24	8	7
Drinks 2 to 3 times a month or less	2	2	15	4	4

Note: Source: 2000 BCS (weighted data). Significant differences are discussed in the text.

Table 2.13: Percentage of respondents aged 16 to 29 using various drugs in the last year by frequency of visits to night clubs

	Cocaine	Ecstasy	Any drug	Hallucinants	Class A
Less than once a week	4	4	22	8	7
At least once a week	8	**10	**39	**16	**14

Note: ** = significant difference at $p<0.01$. Source: 2000 BCS (weighted data).

One last factor associated with drug use concerns health status. While this involves complex issues, it is clear from Table 2.14 that drug users rate their health differently from non-users. A similar pattern emerges for all the various drug types, whereby those reporting their health as 'bad' or 'fair' were more likely than those reporting 'good' or 'very good' health to have used drugs in the last year. A significantly higher percentage of those reporting 'fair' health took any drug ($p<0.01$), ecstasy ($p<0.05$) and hallucinants ($p<0.01$) compared with those rating their health as 'very good'. Whether general health is affected by drug use, drugs are taken to alleviate health problems or health and drug use are both related to other factors is difficult to say. The health risks of drug misuse have been widely documented and although this analysis is based on respondents' own assessment of their health status, it does highlight the importance of considering the link between drugs and health. A more in-depth discussion of these issues can be found in the 1994 BCS report (Ramsay and Percy, 1996).

Table 2.14:   **Percentage of respondents aged 16 to 29 using various drugs in the last year by self-reported general health status**

	Cocaine	Ecstasy	Hallucinants	Any drug	Class A
Very good	4	4	7	20	6
Good	4	5	10	27	8
Fair	7	8	13	36	14
Bad	12	16	18	36	16

Source: BCS 2000 (weighted data). Significant differences are discussed in the text.

Population estimates

National surveys can be used not only to shed light on what kinds of people are more at risk of drug use, but also to provide estimates of the actual number of drug users. Table 2.15 provides estimates of the number of 16- to 29-year-olds who have consumed cocaine, heroin, cannabis, any drug and Class A drugs. Also included are the upper and lower ranges, which are based on 95 per cent confidence intervals[6]. Of the 9.5 million young people aged 16 to 29 in England and Wales, at least 2.3 million have used a prohibited drug in the last year and 1.5 million in the last month. Estimates for cocaine and heroin are considerably lower at 457,000 and 65,000 respectively for use in the last year. Finally, it is estimated that 763,000 young people aged 16 to 29 have used Class A drugs in the last year. For use in the last month, the estimates are approximately half this figure, at 373,000. Equivalent information for 16- to 24-year-olds can be found in Table B.11 in Appendix B.

---

6 The confidence interval is a range of values which we can be confident includes the true value. A 95% confidence interval will therefore not include the true population value 5% of the time (Altman, 1991).

Table 2.15: **Estimates of the number of 16- to 29-year-olds using various drugs in the last year and last month in England and Wales, 2000**

	Best estimate	Lower estimate	Higher estimate
Cocaine			
Number using in the last year	457,000	364,000	572,000
Number using in the last month	178,000	125,000	253,000
Heroin			
Number using in the last year	65,000	37,000	113,000
Number using in the last month	31,000	14,000	71,000
Cannabis			
Number using in the last year	2,115,000	1,901,000	2,330,000
Number using in the last month	1,345,000	1,195,000	1,510,000
Any drug			
Number using in the last year	2,347,000	2,126,000	2,568,000
Number using in the last month	1,475,000	1,317,000	1,647,000
Any Class A drug			
Number using in the last year	763,000	641,000	905,000
Number using in the last month	373,000	292,000	475,000

Note: The upper and lower estimates encompass the 95% confidence range (calculated using a logit transformation for those proportions that are less than 0.2 or greater than 0.8, taking account of the samples' non-normal distribution) together with varying design effects for different drugs. The estimated number of 16- to 29-year-olds in England and Wales is 9.4 million. It should be noted that the estimates used are lower than those for 1998 and previous surveys, as in 1998 the ONS estimate of the number of 16- to 29-year-olds was higher, at approximately 10.4 million. Figures have been rounded to the nearest 1,000. Source 2000 BCS (weighted data), together with ONS 1999 mid-year population estimates.

Summary

This chapter has examined current patterns of drug use among the general population. Rates were generally higher in younger people and in men compared with women. About half of 16- to 29-year-olds had ever used drugs. Rates for more recent periods were much lower at 25 per cent for use in the last year and 16 per cent for use in the last month. Cannabis remains the most commonly consumed drug, with about 44 per cent of young people aged 16 to 29 having used it within their lifetime.

While rates for use in the last year of heroin, crack and (unprescribed) Methadone were found to be low (about 1%), the equivalent figure for cocaine use among 16 to 29s was five times higher. Indeed, the rate for cocaine use among this age group was similar to ecstasy and was even higher in some regions of England and Wales, emphasising its increasing popularity with young people. London was found to have the highest prevalence rates for any drug, cocaine and Class A drugs.

Socio-economic factors were associated with certain types of drug use. One notable feature of this analysis was the contrast between the characteristics of cocaine and heroin users. An analysis by ACORN category showed consistently higher levels of drug use among 16 to 29s in affluent urban areas for any drug, cocaine and Class A drugs. However, this did not hold true for heroin, which was more widespread in the less affluent categories (council estates/low income and new/mature home-owning areas). Similar patterns were observed for income, education, social class and employment status, with heroin use tending to be more prevalent among less advantaged elements of the population.

The importance of the link between drug use and alcohol consumption was highlighted by the higher rates of drug use in those young people who go to pubs more often and who drink more frequently. Rates were also higher in those who attended nightclubs more often.

3   Changing patterns of drug use, 1994 to 2000

One of the major strengths of the data on drug use from the BCS lies in the comparability over time. It remains the only measure of drug use from a random sample of the general household population of England and Wales to be collected on a regular and consistent basis. Data are now available from four sweeps, carried out every other year since 1994.

This chapter concentrates on the changes in drug use observed since 1994, primarily by those aged 16 to 29. This age group continues to experience the greatest levels of and fluctuations in drug use compared with older sections of society. Changes in drug use by those between 16 and 24 years of age, the group most focussed on in the Government's anti-drugs strategy, are covered in Chapter 5.

Previous BCS drugs reports have attempted to examine the process of 'macro' diffusion, namely, the widespread routes involved in the wax and wane of various types of drug use over time, across areas and between broad social groupings (e.g. Ramsay and Partridge, 1999). These analyses have shown clear links between changes in various types of drug use and a range of characteristics such as region, employment status and ACORN category. The broad diffusion model was first conceived of as being useful in a drugs context in the 1970s (Hunt and Chambers, 1976) and has proved an invaluable tool in drugs research since. However, some have argued that the power of the concept could be improved through greater incorporation of economic aspects of drug use, such as availability (Ferrence, 2001).

Changes by age group

The proportion of adults (i.e. all those aged 16 to 59) using any type of drug in the previous year has not altered significantly between 1994 and 2000, as shown in Table 3.1, and remains at around one in ten of the population. However, there were significant increases in use of both powder and crack cocaine in 2000 compared with levels in previous surveys. The absolute number of crack users in the 16 to 59 age group, though, remains very low, so the figures should be handled with care. Use of ecstasy in the last year by 16- to 59-year-olds, however, only rose just enough in 2000 to be significantly different from the 1994 level ($p<0.05$) but not from the 1996 or 1998 levels. The other side to the equation was that rates of amphetamine use in the last year fell in 2000 compared with levels in all three previous sweeps, and LSD usage dropped significantly from its rate in 1994 and 1996. Most of these changes involved quite small figures, and hence some of the proportions appear unchanged when rounded to whole numbers, despite there being a significant difference. For example, rates of crack use in the last year were consistently below 0.5 per cent across the four sweeps but in fact increased by a factor of more than ten (0.03% to 0.32%). For this reason, the figures in Tables 3.1 and 3.2 are shown to one decimal place.

Table 3.1: **Percentage of respondents aged 16 to 59 using various drugs in the last year, 1994–2000**

	1994	1996	1998	2000
Cocaine	**0.5	**0.6	**1.1	1.7
Crack	0.0	**0.1	**0.1	0.3
Heroin	0.2	0.2	0.1	0.3
Amphetamine	*2.4	**2.9	**2.6	1.9
Ecstasy	*1.0	1.4	1.2	1.6
LSD	**1.3	*0.9	0.6	0.6
Cannabis	8.4	8.7	9.0	9.4
Any drug	9.9	10.3	10.5	10.7

Note: * = significantly different from 2000 at $p<0.05$; ** = significantly different from 2000 at $p<0.01$.
Source: 1994, 1996, 1998 and 2000 BCS (weighted data).

The equivalent changes in 2000 compared with previous years for the younger group of adults (16 to 29) were essentially the same as those for the full age range but with more extreme differences (Table 3.2). That is:

- amphetamine and LSD usage fell significantly
- ecstasy use had not increased significantly since 1996
- cannabis and heroin use remained statistically unchanged
- use of cocaine and crack increased significantly.

Table 3.2: Percentage of respondents aged 16 to 29 using various drugs in the last year, 1994–2000

	1994	1996	1998	2000
Cocaine	**1.2	**1.3	*3.1	4.9
Crack	0.0	0.2	*0.2	0.8
Heroin	0.5	0.3	0.3	0.7
Amphetamine	*6.8	**8.2	**7.9	5.2
Ecstasy	**3.0	4.3	3.9	5.0
LSD	**3.9	2.8	2.1	1.9
Cannabis	20.3	21.1	22.5	22.5
Any drug	23.3	24.0	25.2	24.9

Note: * = significantly different from 2000 at $p<0.05$; ** = significantly different from 2000 at $p<0.01$.
Source: 1994, 1996, 1998 and 2000 BCS (weighted data).

16- to 19-year-olds

Although the patterns for all 16- to 29-year-olds do largely reflect those in the full age range, there were important variations within this set of young adults. Turning first to the teenage group in the BCS (i.e. the 16- to 19-year-olds), use of any illicit drug in the last year in 2000 was significantly *lower*, having fallen by a fifth since 1994 (See Table 3.3). This was the result of significant declines in the use of a number of drugs – particularly LSD, poppers and amphetamine. Use of other drugs, such as cannabis, also dropped slightly in the 2000 survey and, whilst not significant in their own right, contributed to the significant overall reduction in the use of 'any drug'.

The decreases in use of LSD (by three-quarters) and amphetamine (by one-half) from their respective peaks in 1994 and 1996 have been at least as dramatic for the 16 to 19 age group as they have been for 16- to 29-year-olds. No doubt this reflects the fall from fashion of these drugs and amphetamine's replacement, to some degree, by cocaine as the stimulant of choice. Use of cocaine is now almost as great for 16- to 19-year-olds as for those in their 20s – previously it had been consumed largely by the latter. Most other research with young drug users has found few teenage users of cocaine, as summarised by Boys and colleagues (2001). This may be due to the historically high price of cocaine, which whilst falling over recent years, remains relatively costly, and restricted access to sources of supply among this younger age group, especially those not able to get into pubs or clubs. Use of other drug types remains unchanged in statistical terms, including ecstasy, although heroin and crack prevalence rates have risen slightly. These latter two drugs were consumed by less than one in 100 of those aged 16 to 19 during the year before their interview in the 2000 survey.

Table 3.3: *Percentage of respondents aged 16 to 19 using various drugs in the last year, 1994–2000*

	1994	1996	1998	2000
Cocaine	*1	1	*1	4
Crack	0	-	-	1
Heroin	1	-	-	1
Amphetamine	*10	**11	9	6
Ecstasy	5	6	4	5
LSD	**8	*5	2	2
Poppers	*7	5	4	4
Cannabis	29	27	28	25
Any drug	*34	31	31	27

Note: * = significantly different from 2000 at *p*<0.05; ** = significantly different from 2000 at *p*<0.01.
Source: 1994, 1996, 1998 and 2000 BCS (weighted data). '-' = less than 0.5% (this convention is used in the rest of the tables in this chapter).

On examination of the figures for men and women (see Table 3.4), there were no significant changes over time in the use of 'any drug' or of cocaine among 16- to 19-year-olds. Nonetheless, the 2000 figures for 'any drug' were lower than their 1994 equivalents across all three recall periods for both sexes. The reduction in lifetime use of 'any drug' between 1998 and 2000 by men was larger, though – it fell by 20 per cent, compared with only a five per cent drop for women over the same time period. Conversely, cocaine use was higher over the three recall periods in 2000 than previously for both sexes – rising by a factor of six from levels in 1994 and 1996.

Table 3.4: *Percentage of respondents aged 16 to 19 using cocaine and 'any drug' in their lifetime, the last year and last month by sex, 1994–2000*

	Men				Women			
	1994	1996	1998	2000	1994	1996	1998	2000
Cocaine								
Lifetime	3	3	4	8	3	-	2	4
Last year	1	1	2	6	1	-	-	2
Last month	-	-	-	3	1	-	0	1
Any drug								
Lifetime	48	48	55	44	45	42	42	40
Last year	39	35	35	31	30	27	26	24
Last month	25	23	25	21	16	15	19	12

Source: 1994, 1996, 1998 and 2000 BCS (weighted data).

20- to 24-year-olds

Within the 20- to 24-year-old group, use within the last year of any illicit drug and of cannabis has risen consistently throughout the series thus far (see Table 3.5), but neither were significantly higher in 2000 than before. Indeed, on comparison of the 2000 with the 1998 results, it can be seen that there has been remarkably little change, with only the steep reduction in amphetamine use achieving any level of significance. An important finding was that cocaine use did not continue to rise to the same degree as that seen between 1996 and 1998 (when the increase was statistically significant at $p<0.05$). Cocaine use may conceivably have plateaued in this age group, just as ecstasy appears to have stabilised since 1996. It is too early, however, to comment with any authority on trends in use of these drugs, and further careful monitoring of changes in the (now annual) BCS data will be necessary.

Use of unprescribed tranquillisers has risen for the second survey in a row, though this relatively modest increase should be treated circumspectly, as the differences between 2000 compared with levels in previous years were not statistically significant. The (significant) rise in the use of crack by 2000 on 1994 levels should be regarded in a similar fashion, although this is also a possible warning that use of this potentially damaging drug is growing. Further qualitative research with these young users of crack and tranquillisers would aid our understanding of the meaning and context of these changes. In addition, extended survey questions on the frequency of use, for example, would assist judgements on how far use of drugs was occasional or recreational, as opposed to habitual or out of control.

Recent research by Boys et al. (2001) found that in their non-treatment, non-criminal justice system based sample of drug users, some reported using crack occasionally. Furthermore, some of these had not been aware that it was crack until the interviewer had clearly described its properties – if users usually smoked rather than sniffed cocaine, as seems to be the case for some, this could have been an easy mistake to make. The converse may also be true; it is feasible that some reports of crack use in the BCS were, in truth, smoked powder cocaine or freebase (Bean, 1993: p.4). "Crack is not a new drug but a new delivery system for cocaine", as was commented when reports of its use first emerged in this country (Gossop et al., 1994). There have also been recent reports of dealers selling crack to clubbers who were in search of powder cocaine and advising them that they should crush the rocks of crack in order to snort them more easily ('Clubbers lured into using crack cocaine', Independent, 19 April 2001).

Table 3.5: **Percentage of respondents aged 20 to 24 using various drugs in the last year, 1994–2000**

	1994	1996	1998	2000
Cocaine	**1	**2	5	6
Crack	-	-	-	1
Heroin	1	-	-	1
Amphetamine	8	**11	*10	6
Ecstasy	*3	6	5	6
LSD	3	3	3	2
Tranquillisers	1	-	1	2
Cannabis	23	24	26	27
Any drug	25	27	28	30

Note: * = significantly different from 2000 at p<0.05; ** = significantly different from 2000 at p<0.01.
Source: 1994, 1996, 1998 and 2000 BCS (weighted data).

There were some interesting variations over time by sex in the 20 to 24 age group, especially when focussing on drugs used within the lifetime of respondents in addition to drugs they had taken in the last year (Table 3.6). The data were consistent with stable levels for at least 'trying' amphetamine – probably for the majority of users initially during mid to late adolescence (Parker et al., 1998). It is difficult to make clear statements about this aspect as the age of first use is not known, although this information will be available from 2001 onwards for those aged 16 to 24. Nevertheless, it seems that the decline in the popularity of amphetamine has primarily affected rates of continuation in use for young men of this age group over time, rather than the lifetime (or 'trying') rates.

Clearly, when we compare age groups across time, we are not considering the same cohorts of people – those who were aged 20 to 24 in 1994 are now six years older – but it will take time for lifetime rates to fall, providing today's teenagers continue to be relatively abstemious. For women, use of amphetamine within their lifetime was significantly higher in 2000 compared with 1994 and 1996, but last year rates remained low and unchanged. This suggests that women were never using amphetamine as often as men were, but have now tried it in similar proportions in this age group. A similar effect, though operating in reverse, appears to exist for cannabis. Against a backdrop of fairly hefty increases in lifetime rates for both sexes, use in the last year by women rose from 17 to 24 per cent, compared with a relatively flat rate for men (29% to 30%) between 1994 and 2000.

One in ten men aged 20 to 24 in the 2000 BCS reported ever trying tranquillisers that were not prescribed for them, which was a massive rise on the levels found in any other BCS[7]. This was the only significant change between 1998 and 2000 for either sex in this age group – there was no such increase in unprescribed tranquilliser use by women. Another important factor was that tranquilliser misuse appeared to be clustered into reasonably discrete groups. For example, of all those who had misused tranquillisers in the last year (n=86), around 30 per cent were men under 30 years of age but about 20 per cent were women aged 40 to 59.

Table 3.6: *Percentage of respondents aged 20 to 24 using various drugs in their lifetime and the last year by sex, 1994–2000*

	Men				Women			
	1994	1996	1998	2000	1994	1996	1998	2000
Cocaine								
Lifetime	**4	9	13	16	**2	**3	7	11
Last year	**2	*3	5	8	1	1	4	4
Amphetamine								
Lifetime	*19	26	27	27	**13	**16	22	28
Last year	*12	**17	12	6	6	6	8	6
Ecstasy								
Lifetime	*11	19	15	19	**6	8	11	12
Last year	4	11	7	8	3	3	5	3
Tranquillisers								
Lifetime	**4	*4	**3	10	3	3	3	2
Last year	2	1	1	3	1	-	1	1
Cannabis								
Lifetime	**42	48	57	55	**30	**36	41	49
Last year	29	29	34	30	17	20	20	24
Any drug								
Lifetime	**51	57	64	63	**38	*43	48	54
Last year	31	32	37	34	20	23	22	26

Note: * = significantly different from 2000 at $p<0.05$; ** = significantly different from 2000 at $p<0.01$.
Source: 1994, 1996, 1998 and 2000 BCS (weighted data).

---

7 The 95% confidence interval for the proportion ever using tranquillisers in the 2000 BCS was six to 14 per cent.

25- to 29-year-olds

There was relatively little change between 1998 and 2000 in the prevalence of drug use within the 25 to 29 age group (Table 3.7). The recent doubling of rates of ecstasy use within the last year for men is worthy of comment, however – especially as use of this drug among 16- to 24-year-olds has not altered significantly since 1996. This probably reflects the continuing use of ecstasy by an older hardcore of club-going men. This was the cohort who would have been in their late teens or very early twenties in the first part of the 1990s, when the rave phenomenon led to dramatic changes in drug use among young people (Collin, 1997).

Cocaine use, however, is now as common as ecstasy use among this age group but, as was the case for 20- to 24-year-olds, the increase in consumption of cocaine from 1998 to 2000 was not significant. This is a further sign that growth in the use of cocaine may not be continuing to accelerate. Changes in the use of more harmful substances in the last year, such as crack and heroin, were not significant. Nonetheless, the net result of these small changes in the prevalence of different drugs was that overall rates for 'any drug' remained a third higher than in 1994 for 25- to 29-year-olds (both sexes together). However, none of the changes for women were statistically significant, indicating that women continue to 'grow out' of drug use earlier than men do.

Table 3.7: Percentage of respondents aged 25 to 29 using various drugs in the last year by sex, 1994–2000

	1994	1996	1998	2000
Cocaine				
Men	1	**1	5	8
Women	1	2	2	2
All	**1	**1	3	5
Ecstasy				
Men	**2	**3	*4	8
Women	1	2	1	1
All	**1	**2	*2	4
Cannabis				
Men	**17	19	25	23
Women	8	11	10	12
All	*12	15	16	17
Any drug				
Men	*19	22	28	26
Women	11	13	11	14
All	**15	17	19	20

Note: * = significantly different from 2000 at p<0.05; ** = significantly different from 2000 at p<0.01.
Source: 1994, 1996, 1998 and 2000 BCS (weighted data).

Regional variations

It has previously been suggested that fashions involving drug use customarily begin among pockets of users in specific metropolitan areas (Ramsay and Partridge, 1999). 'Urban clustering' is a related phenomenon for heroin diffusion, namely the way in which problems associated with the sale and use of heroin tend to become concentrated in certain deprived neighbourhoods within cities (Pearson and Gilman, 1994). On a broader, regional basis, prior BCS analyses have shown markedly higher prevalence rates in London and, to a lesser degree, parts of the North West. For example, cocaine use was much higher in London and Merseyside than in other regions in the 1998 BCS.

Similar disparities were also apparent in the 2000 data, which point to one in nine young adults in London using cocaine in the year before interview – more than double the levels found anywhere else. Table 3.8 shows these latest changes in the use of cocaine in the last year, alongside those for amphetamine and 'any drug', for 16- to 29-year-olds. These figures provide further evidence that increases in cocaine use may not be proceeding at the same rate in all areas of the country – only the North showed a significant rise on 1998 levels. The rate of increase has slowed in London, the South and Anglia, while use has risen at least three-fold in the other regions of England and Wales (i.e. the North, Wales and the Midlands). However, reductions within several regions in use of amphetamine (significant only in the North and the South) and other drugs have contributed to the absence of any net, significant changes to illicit drug use overall within the last year. As mentioned earlier in this report, the rise in the popularity of cocaine has partly taken place at the same time as a decrease in the appeal of amphetamine to young people (Boys *et al.*, 2001). This phenomenon has not occurred at the same rate in all areas of the country, however.

Table 3.8: *Percentage of respondents aged 16 to 29 using cocaine, amphetamine and any drug in the last year by region, 1994–2000*

	1994	1996	1998	2000
Cocaine				
North	**1	**1	*1	4
Anglia	1	-	4	5
Wales	1	0	1	3
London	**4	**4	9	11
South	-	**2	4	5
Midlands	1	1	-	3
England & Wales	**1	**1	*3	5
Amphetamine				
North	8	*10	9	6
Anglia	8	7	2	5
Wales	7	9	6	5
London	8	6	8	4
South	6	*8	*8	4
Midlands	6	8	7	5
England & Wales	*7	**8	**8	5
Any drug				
North	22	26	26	26
Anglia	22	22	19	28
Wales	27	15	17	19
London	32	29	32	31
South	25	26	25	24
Midlands	16	18	21	21
England & Wales	23	24	25	25

Note: * = significantly different from 2000 at $p<0.05$; ** = significantly different from 2000 at $p<0.01$.
Source: 1994, 1996, 1998 and 2000 BCS (weighted data).

Employment status

Over the last half of the 1990s, rates of unemployment among 16- to 29-year-olds fell fairly steadily in England and Wales from ten per cent of the labour force in 1994 to seven per cent by 1998 (source: ONS Labour Force Survey). There have also been shifts in the relationships between use of certain drugs and employment status. These changes in use of cocaine, heroin, LSD, magic mushrooms and 'any drug' by young people within the last year are outlined in Table 3.9 below. As the majority of this age group were employed in each survey, it was not surprising that the changes for those in work largely reflected changes for the group as a whole. For example, there has been a steady rise in the use of cocaine since 1996 by those in work and (more recently) the economically inactive. Levels of cocaine use in 2000 did not differ by employment status, whereas in 1998, for example, the rate of use among the unemployed was double that of those working. Examinations of the differences in drug use by employment status can be found in Chapter 2 for 2000 data and previous BCS drugs reports for earlier years (e.g. Ramsay and Partridge, 1999: p.51).

There were no significant changes over time for use of heroin, but rates of use of this drug in the last year for the unemployed were noticeably higher in 1998 and 2000 than for those in work or classified as economically inactive. Other analyses of pre-2000 BCS data found little to support a relationship between occupational attainment (in terms of the average hourly wages of the respondent's occupation, based on the UK Quarterly Labour Force Survey) and drug use. It did, however, find 'compelling evidence' that cocaine use particularly was associated with unemployment (MacDonald and Pudney, 2000). It would be worth reconsidering this conclusion in the light of the evidence from the latest BCS.

Another change in 2000 has been the dramatic reduction in the use of hallucinogens (i.e. LSD and magic mushrooms) by the young unemployed. Whereas in 1996, one in eight unemployed young people had tried LSD in the previous year, by 2000 only one in 100 had done so[8]. The shift may reflect the findings of some recent, qualitative research (Measham et al., 1998: p.13), where LSD and magic mushrooms (along with solvents and poppers) had come to be regarded by young interviewees as 'early experimentation' drugs, grown out of by mid-teens and seen as causing immature or antisocial behaviour. In contrast, use of hallucinogens by the employed has remained at the same, low levels across the whole series of surveys.

---

8 However, because the numbers using these drugs among the unemployed is now so small, the statistical tests comparing 2000 with previous years become unreliable (See Appendix E).

Table 3.9: Percentage of respondents aged 16 to 29 using various drugs in the last year by employment status, 1994–2000

	1994	1996	1998	2000
Cocaine				
Unemployed	2	3	6	4
Employed	1	**1	*3	5
Inactive	2	**1	2	5
Heroin				
Unemployed	1	1	4	3
Employed	0	-	0	-
Inactive	1	-	-	1
LSD				
Unemployed	10	12	5	1
Employed	2	2	2	2
Inactive	**6	3	2	2
Mushrooms				
Unemployed	6	5	8	1
Employed	2	1	2	2
Inactive	3	2	3	2
Any drug				
Unemployed	34	45	40	33
Employed	*20	23	25	25
Inactive	26	23	23	22

Note: * = significantly different from 2000 at p<0.05; ** = significantly different from 2000 at p<0.01.
Source: 1994, 1996, 1998 and 2000 BCS (weighted data).

ACORN categories

What kinds of area do the 'new cocaine users' live in and has this changed since 1994? If we examine the alterations in rates of cocaine use in the last year for young adults by ACORN[9] category (Table 3.10), we can see evidence of the broad processes of diffusion at work. In all four surveys, cocaine use has been highest among those living in affluent urban areas. However, the biggest increases in cocaine use were not seen most recently, but between 1996 and 1998 for all areas apart from council estate/low income and affluent family areas, where the most recent upsurges from 1998 to 2000 were the greatest in magnitude. This may represent a degree of harmonisation in the prevalence of cocaine use outside affluent urban areas.

9 The ACORN classification system is briefly outlined in Chapter 2.

Table 3.10: Percentage of respondents aged 16 to 29 using cocaine in the last year by ACORN classification, 1994–2000

	1994	1996	1998	2000
Affluent suburban and rural areas	1	1	5	5
Affluent family areas	0	1	-	3
Affluent urban areas	**3	*4	7	11
Mature home-owning areas	1	**1	2	4
New home-owning areas	2	1	3	5
Council estates and low income areas	*1	*1	2	4

Note: * = significantly different from 2000 at $p<0.05$; ** = significantly different from 2000 at $p<0.01$.
Source: 1994, 1996, 1998 and 2000 BCS (weighted data).

Conclusion

Probably *the* crucial feature highlighted by the series of BCS sweeps from 1994 to 2000 is the increase in use of powder cocaine by young men. This is even more startling for occurring, as it has, against a backdrop of relative stability in other drug use and declines for particular drugs, such as amphetamine. Indeed, for the younger, teenage group, the overall rate of use of any illicit drug appears to be on the decrease – falling by a significant margin from 1994 levels for the first time.

The decisions by young people to use illicit drugs are based on a complex assessment of the risks, costs and benefits involved (Parker *et al.*, 1998). Perceptions of the relative costs and benefits of taking cocaine compared with amphetamine appear to have shifted in favour of the former over the last few years of the 1990s. A decline in the cost of cocaine by almost one-half since 1994, after adjusting for inflation (Corkery, 2000), may well have been an important contributory factor in the diffusion of cocaine use beyond its traditional core.

With the increased overall sample size in the latest BCS and the growth in use of cocaine, it becomes possible to look at the characteristics of users in more detail. It is important to assess who and where these 'new cocaine users' are, so that targeted information and education strategies are in place to anticipate and cope with any rises in demand for treatment or other assistance. Already, the proportion of those presenting for treatment who admit misusing cocaine has increased by 70 per cent since 1993 (Department of Health, 2000). Furthermore, there has been a dramatic rise in the number of recorded cocaine-related deaths, from 12 in 1993 to 50 in 1998 – an increase of more than four-fold (Corkery, 2000). However, major public health problems related to the increased use of powder cocaine may take some time to come to the fore, as cocaine users have generally delayed seeking help or treatment until they experience serious difficulties associated with their drug use (Haynes *et al.*, 2000).

It is difficult to extrapolate future trends and patterns in the use of drugs, especially on the back of only four data points. However, the evidence presented here indicates that the use of cocaine may be approaching a peak, at least among 'trend-setting' groups such as young Londoners, where increases from 1998 to 2000 were no longer statistically significant, as they were for previous years. This is consistent with the "S-shaped" curve associated with epidemics of heroin use (Hunt and Chambers, 1976; Ditton and Frischer, 2001) and diffusion of substance use behaviour more generally (Ferrence, 2001). By the same token, use of cocaine appears to be increasing more rapidly among young people in other sections of society where previously signs of use were virtually absent, such as those in stable employment or living in new home-owning areas.

It must be kept in mind, however, that any general household survey will always underestimate illegal activities such as drug use, and particularly use of those drugs with the greatest taboos associated with their use (White and Lewis, 1998). Hence, some of the increase in the use of cocaine could conceivably reflect an increased willingness to report consumption of what has become a fashionable commodity. The converse may also be true, as suggested by Wish and colleagues (1997), with reference to evidence that the increasing stigmatisation of drug use in the US over recent decades has tended to depress survey disclosure rates. Furthermore, it is by no means inevitable that rates of cocaine use will eventually decrease. There will be more confidence in whether cocaine use is peaking if data from 2001 confirm decelerating usage among certain important groups of young people.

4   Ethnic comparisons

Drug use across ethnic groups has previously been described in the 1994 and 1996 British Crime Survey reports (Ramsay and Percy, 1996; Ramsay and Spiller, 1997). This chapter covers similar ground. It describes ethnic minority participation rates and provides a summary of patterns of use of particular drugs by ethnic groups from the 2000 BCS. There is also a comparison of drug-taking within ethnic groups across the 1994, 1996 and 2000 surveys. Appendix C provides more detailed data on prevalence rates and non-response.

Sample size and participation rates

The main ethnic groups compared in this chapter are white, all black groups, Indian and Pakistani/Bangladeshi. The category of 'all black groups' was referred to in previous BCS reports as 'Afro-Caribbean'. Then and now, this covers 'Black Caribbean', 'Black African' and 'Black Other' categories. The new term has been adopted to more appropriately reflect the heterogeneity of this group and to be consistent with the most recent BCS reports on non-drug related topics.

People from minority ethnic groups account for a small proportion of the population in England and Wales; the 1998 ONS Labour Force Survey estimate for those aged 16–59 was six per cent. Thus, even very large random sample surveys generate minority sub-groups that are too small to permit detailed analysis. For this reason, the BCS has incorporated 'booster samples' of the larger minority ethnic groups. The 2000 BCS was the largest survey in the series to date, with a national core sample of 19,411 respondents, and an additional ethnic booster sample of 3,874. The total sample included 18,355 white people, 1,773 black people; 1,437 Indians; 1,058 Pakistani and Bangladeshi respondents and 603 persons of mixed race or other ethnic group (there were 59 cases where ethnic group was missing). These figures are for the complete sample; only those aged under 60 were asked to complete the drugs self-report component (see Table A.19 in Appendix A).

The booster sample was assembled partly by over-sampling in areas with high densities of minority ethnic groups, and partly through a process of 'focused enumeration' whereby respondents were selected from homes adjacent to those of core respondents if they were from ethnic minorities. In the 2000 BCS, the response rate for the core sample was 74 per cent, and for the booster sample 58 per cent. Full details of the sampling methodology, and other aspects of the survey design, can be found in Hales *et al.* (2000). The main findings on crime and victimisation from the 2000 BCS are in Kershaw *et al.* (2000).

Participation rates for the drugs component of the 2000 BCS were 98 per cent for whites; 96 per cent for black people; 92 per cent for Indians, and 81 per cent for Pakistani/Bangladeshis. These rates were a modest improvement, at least for some minority ethnic groups, from the levels of participation in 1996 (98% for whites; 94% for black people; 86% for Indians and 78% for Pakistani/Bangladeshis). A greater proportion of respondents received assistance from the interviewer in 2000 than in 1996, although this was a smaller proportion in 2000 than in 1994 (Table 4.1).

Table 4.1: ***Percentage accepting or refusing to participate in the drugs self-report questions by ethnic group, 1994, 1996 and 2000***

	White	All black groups	Indian	Pakistani/ Bangladeshi
Accepted (not helped)				
1994 BCS	90.4	75.2	76.2	55.3
1996 BCS	94.1	86.7	79.0	65.4
2000 BCS	92.7	87.3	79.9	67.8
Accepted (needed help)				
1994 BCS	7.7	18.0	14.1	15.5
1996 BCS	4.2	7.2	7.5	12.6
2000 BCS	5.8	8.6	12.3	12.9
TOTAL ACCEPTED				
1994 BCS	98.1	93.2	90.3	70.8
1996 BCS	98.3	93.9	86.5	78.0
2000 BCS	98.5	95.9	92.2	80.7
Refused to participate				
1994 BCS	1.9	6.8	9.7	29.2
1996 BCS	1.7	6.1	13.5	22.0
2000 BCS	1.5	4.1	7.8	19.3

Source: 1994, 1996 and 2000 core and booster samples of BCS (weighted data).

There has been some suggestion that Asian drug use may be 'hidden' from official statistics due to under-reporting of drug use (Pearson and Patel, 1998). In the 2000 BCS, 19 per cent of Pakistani/Bangladeshis refused to participate in the drugs self-report questionnaire. Of this group, nearly two-thirds were women and over two-thirds were aged between 30 and 59 years – therefore having demographic characteristics associated with a relatively low likelihood of drug-taking. However, we should not be complacent about the potential for non-response bias. For example, any under-reporting of drug use in Asian women would pose a challenge to the identification of any new diffusion of drug use into this sub-group. The commonest reasons for non-participation given by Pakistanis and Bangladeshis suggest that language difficulties may have been the main problem. This reason was cited by nearly two-thirds (64%) of Pakistani/Bangladeshi non-respondents.

Differential reporting can be further examined by looking at the 'Don't Want to Answer' (DWA) option. As with previous reports, refusing to answer occurred to a modest extent, with two per cent of whites and Pakistani/Bangladeshis and three per cent of Indians and black people refusing to answer the question on lifetime use of cannabis, for example. DWAs assume greater importance for the more stigmatised drugs, such as heroin and crack. For example, 0.4 per cent of white people refused to answer the question on lifetime use of heroin compared to 1.1 per cent of Pakistani/Bangladeshis, 1.7 per cent of Indians and 1.0 per cent of black people. A similar pattern can be seen concerning lifetime rates of crack use. Refusal to answer this question among whites was 0.4 per cent, compared to 1.5 per cent of Pakistani/ Bangladeshis, 2.1 per cent of Indians and 1.5 per cent of black people. As in previous reports, the proportions refusing to answer questions on lifetime use of heroin and crack were not dissimilar to those for the self-reported rates. This may have important implications, in that self-reported drug use could be an under-estimate of the true prevalence rate in the various ethnic populations, if refusals were, in fact, largely because respondents *had* used the drug in question.

Further information on DWA responses is contained in Appendix C, Tables C.2 and C3. In this report, as in the equivalent ones for 1994 and 1996, only those respondents reporting use of drugs, as opposed to those opting for DWA, have been counted as consumers (DWAs are in fact recoded as 'no' responses).

Self-reported drug taking by ethnic groups

Lifetime prevalence rates are presented separately for the full age range (16–59), the younger group (16–29) and older respondents (30–59). As in previous reports, this chapter presents tables of the self-reported use of the illegal drugs most widely consumed in the UK (cannabis and amphetamine, together with cocaine and ecstasy) and those with dependence potential and/or a possible link to crime (heroin and crack).[10] Prevalence rates are also presented for use of Class A drugs and any drug.

---

10   The NEW-ADAM programme reported that 29 per cent of arrestees tested positive for opiates (including heroin) and 20 per cent tested positive for cocaine (including crack) (Bennett, 2000).

Table 4.2 summarises lifetime experience of drugs by different ethnic groups aged 16 to 59. Cannabis was by far the most common drug taken at some point in people's lives, irrespective of ethnicity. However, drug use was less prevalent among the different ethnic minority groups in comparison to whites, particularly in the Asian community. Lifetime use of any drug reached to over a third (34%) in white people compared to 28 per cent among black respondents, 15 per cent of Indians and ten per cent of Pakistani/Bangladeshis. The prevalence in the mixed ethnicity group is discussed later in the chapter.

Table 4.2: **Percentage of respondents aged 16 to 59 using various drugs in their lifetime by ethnic group**

	White	All black groups	Indian	Pakistani/ Bangladeshi	Mixed ethnicity
Cocaine	5	3	3	*1	6
Crack	1	2	1	-	2
Heroin	1	1	-	-	2
Amphetamine	*12	**7	**3	**1	17
Ecstasy	**5	**3	**2	**1	11
Cannabis	**28	**24	**10	**6	42
Class A	12	**6	**5	**2	12
Any drug	**34	**28	**15	**10	48

Note: *=significantly different from mixed ethnicity group at $p<0.05$; **=significantly different from mixed ethnicity group at $p<0.01$. Data on the Chinese ethnic group are not included due to small numbers in the sample (n=50). '-' = less than 0.5% (this convention is used in the rest of the tables in this chapter). Source: 2000 BCS, core and booster samples (weighted data).

Among those aged 16 to 29 (Table 4.3), the prevalence of drug use was higher across all the largest ethnic groups, with nearly half (46%) of all white people reporting ever taking cannabis and nearly a quarter (22%) ever using any Class A drug. With the exception of crack, young white people consistently had higher prevalence rates for all the types of lifetime drug use shown in this table. Lifetime use of heroin, cocaine, ecstasy and amphetamine by the Indian ethnic group equated to or exceeded that of young black people. Pakistani/Bangladeshi lifetime drug use rates remained low in comparison to other ethnic groups.

Table 4.3: **Percentage of respondents aged 16 to 29 using various drugs in their lifetime by ethnic group**

	White	All black groups	Indian	Pakistani/ Bangladeshi
Cocaine	10	6	7	1
Crack	2	3	2	-
Heroin	2	-	1	-
Amphetamine	**23	6	6	2
Ecstasy	**12	5	7	2
Cannabis	**46	32	21	9
Class A	**22	9	9	3
Any drug	**52	37	25	13

Note: **=significant difference between whites and all other main ethnic groups at p<0.01. Data on the Chinese ethnic group are not included due to small numbers in the sample (n=50). Source: 2000 BCS, core and booster samples (weighted data).

Table 4.4: **Percentage of respondents aged 30 to 59 using various drugs in their lifetime by ethnic group**

	White	All black groups	Indian	Pakistani/ Bangladeshi
Cocaine	3	2	1	1
Crack	1	1	-	0
Heroin	1	1	0	0
Amphetamine	**8	4	1	1
Ecstasy	2	2	-	-
Cannabis	22	20	4	2
Class A	**8	5	2	2
Any drug	**28	24	9	8

Note: **=significant difference between whites and all other main ethnic groups at p<0.01. Data on the Chinese ethnic group are not included due to small numbers in the sample (n=50). Source: 2000 BCS, core and booster samples (weighted data).

If one examines the prevalence rates of older respondents aged 30 to 59 (Table 4.4), a slightly different pattern emerges. White people have only slightly higher rates of use for any drug and for drugs such as cannabis in comparison to all black groups. Asian drug use in this age group was at least a third of white drug use. Lifetime rates among the Indian and Pakistani/Bangladeshi groups, at least for 30- to 59-year-olds, were very similar.

As in previous surveys, whites had a higher lifetime prevalence of drug use than did other ethnic groups. This applies to the three age groups (16–29, 30–59 and 16–59) for cannabis, amphetamine, cocaine and Class A drugs. There has been a consistent pattern over time in BCS reports whereby drug use is more commonly reported by whites than by black people who, in turn, have a higher reported level of use than Indians and Pakistanis/Bangladeshis. Indeed, the data in Tables 4.2 to 4.4 strongly suggest that, irrespective of age, lifetime experimentation with drugs is more prevalent among white people than other ethnic groups. However, the assumption that Asian drug use is naturally lower than that of other ethnic groups may be challenged by the findings presented in Table 4.3. Here, among 16- to 29-year-olds, lifetime use of drugs such as heroin, cocaine, amphetamine and ecstasy by the young Indian group has reached or even exceeded equivalent levels for young black people (although use of any drug remains lower).

Significance tests have been applied to the data in Tables 4.2 to 4.4 to test the hypotheses that: (1) a greater proportion of whites than any other ethnic group use drugs; and (2) prevalence is ranked from highest to lowest from whites to blacks to Indians to Pakistanis/Bangladeshis. Regarding the first hypothesis, drug use in whites was higher than all other groups to a statistically significant degree for cannabis, amphetamine, ecstasy, Class A drugs and any drug in the 16–59 and 16–29 age groups ($p<0.01$). Also, whites in the 30–59 age group had the highest lifetime prevalence for amphetamine, Class A drugs and any drug ($p<0.01$).

The hypothesis that one might assign ranks to ethnic groups in terms of drug use prevalence was only supported by significance tests for amphetamine and for any drug in the 16–59 age group ($p<0.01$) and for cannabis and any drug in the 16–29 age group ($p<0.01$). No significant pattern of prevalence gradation is present in the 30–59 age group.

The availability of a large data-set bearing on ethnic minorities' drug use in England and Wales means that, for the first time, light can be shed on levels of drug use across a wider range of ethnic categories, including the 'mixed' group. Data relating to lifetime prevalence among white, black, Indian, Pakistani/Bangladeshi and mixed ethnicity groups for the 16–59 group have already been presented in Table 4.2.

The main finding of interest is that prevalence rates for those of 'mixed' ethnicity tended to match or even exceed those of all other ethnic groups, including whites. Although not included in Table 4.4, the proportion of Black Africans using certain drugs was lower than in 'Black Caribbean' and 'Black Other' groups, although some of the absolute differences were small. As already noted, differences in drug use can be observed between Indian, Pakistani and Bangladeshi groups. Greater sensitivity to differences within ethnic minority groups may provide important information on trends in drug use that can be 'hidden' within aggregated categories. Furthermore, it has been suggested that closer examination of ethnic minority drug use may indicate a form of 'early warning' of future problematic usage, including uptake into treatment (Ramsay, 1999).

Comparison of successive surveys

Drug use by ethnic group and by year has been compared between the 1994 and 1996 BCS sweeps (Ramsay and Spiller, 1997). There was no ethnic boost in the 1998 BCS. This section compares results from the 1994 and 1996 sweeps with the current findings for use during the lifetime of respondents and use in the last year. A comparison of drug use by ethnic group, age and survey is shown in Tables 4.5 to 4.7 below.

Lifetime use

Lifetime use of specific drugs in the 16–29 age group from the BCS 1994–2000 is shown in Table 4.5. Whites are the only group with a significant increase in the proportion of respondents reporting the use of cannabis and amphetamine. There was no significant change in lifetime use of heroin for any ethnic group. However, there were tentative warning signs in the form of a rise from one per cent to two per cent for the white 16- to 29-year-old group and a rise from 0 per cent to one per cent for young Indian people. (The unrounded figures are an increase from 0.8 per cent to 1.6 per cent for whites between 1994 and 2000 and an increase from 0 per cent to one per cent for Indian respondents over the same period.) This rise in heroin use among Indians may help explain a rise in heroin smoking reported by young Asian men entering drug treatment services, especially in parts of London (Sondhi et al., 1999).

Lifetime use of cocaine was reported by a higher percentage of white and Indian respondents in 2000 than in 1994 and 1996. In black respondents, lifetime use of cocaine in 2000 was more commonly reported in 2000 than in 1996. Lifetime prevalence of ecstasy rose in the white and Indian groups, and use of crack grew also in the Indian group. The reported lifetime prevalence of crack, cocaine and heroin in the Pakistani/Bangladeshi population was down since the last two surveys, although this was not statistically significant.

Trends in lifetime prevalence may be further assessed in Table 4.6, concerning lifetime use of any drug from 1994 to 2000 for both 16–29 and 16–59 age groups. There was a statistically significant change among white people in both age categories. Lifetime prevalence also increased significantly from 1996 for 16- to 59-year-old black people, and from 1994 for Indians. The decline in lifetime use for Pakistani/Bangladeshis was also significant from 1994 to 2000.

Table 4.5: *Percentage of 16- to 29-year-olds using various drugs in their lifetime by ethnic group, 1994, 1996 and 2000*

	1994	1996	2000
Cocaine			
White	**3	**3	10
All black groups	3	*2	6
Indian	**1	**2	7
Pakistani/Bangladeshi	4	2	1
Crack			
White	-	1	2
All black groups	1	1	3
Indian	**-	**-	2
Pakistani/Bangladeshi	3	-	-
Heroin			
White	1	1	2
All black groups	-	1	-
Indian	0	0	1
Pakistani/Bangladeshi	4	-	-
Amphetamine			
White	**14	**17	23
All black groups	8	7	6
Indian	4	4	6
Pakistani/Bangladeshi	3	2	2
Ecstasy			
White	**6	**9	12
All black groups	7	7	5
Indian	**1	**2	7
Pakistani/Bangladeshi	4	1	2
Cannabis			
White	**34	**38	46
All black groups	27	26	32
Indian	13	18	21
Pakistani/Bangladeshi	12	11	9

Note: *=significantly different from 2000 at $p<0.05$; **=significantly different from 2000 at $p<0.01$. Source: 1994, 1996 and 2000 BCS, core and booster samples (weighted data).

Table 4.6: **Percentage of respondents using any drug in their lifetime by age and ethnic group, 1994, 1996 and 2000**

	1994	1996	2000
16–29 age group			
White	**43	**46	52
All black groups	34	31	37
Indian	19	22	25
Pakistani/Bangladeshi	18	16	13
16–59 age group			
White	**29	**30	34
All black groups	29	*23	28
Indian	**11	14	15
Pakistani/Bangladeshi	**15	12	10

Note: *=significantly different from 2000 at p<0.05; **=significantly different from 2000 at p<0.01
Source: 1994, 1996 and 2000 BCS, core and booster samples (weighted data).

Use in the last year

As shown in Table 4.7, changes in use of any drug in the last year, by the younger age group across the three BCS sweeps, were not statistically significant except for the Indian population. For the 16–59 age group, significant increases are noted for whites from 1994 and 1996 and for all black groups from 1996.

Table 4.7 Percentage of respondents using any drug in the last year by age and ethnic group, 1994, 1996 and 2000

	1994	1996	2000
16–29 age group			
White	24	25	26
All black groups	18	19	21
Indian	*7	10	12
Pakistani/Bangladeshi	8	10	8
16-59 age group			
White	**10	*10	11
All black groups	12	*10	13
Indian	4	5	5
Pakistani/Bangladeshi	5	6	5

Note: *=significantly different from 2000 at p<0.05; **=significantly different from 2000 at p<0.01
Source: 1994, 1996 and 2000 BCS, core and booster samples (weighted data).

Conclusion

The data presented in this chapter show that, irrespective of age, lifetime prevalence was greatest for white people, followed by black then Indian and Pakistani/Bangladeshi groups. In addition, the above analysis identifies the 'mixed' category as an ethnic group who reported very high rates of lifetime drug use. Within these generalisations, it is possible to discern some more specific signs of changes in drug use by ethnic groups. For example, this chapter has been able to point to a decline in the prevalence of drug use among Pakistani/Bangladeshis from the 1994 sweep, for a range of different types of drugs. The prevalence of cocaine use (at least among those aged between 16–29) has significantly increased over time for white, black and Indian groups from the earlier sweeps of the BCS. A particularly striking finding was the seven per cent lifetime prevalence rate of cocaine use by young Indians aged 16–29 in the 2000 BCS, compared with a rate of just two per cent in 1996.

5   Tracking the progress of the anti-drugs strategy

The anti-drugs strategy

In tackling drugs, as in many other policy areas, there is currently a strong emphasis on pursuing quantified targets, rather than just broader aims and objectives. Whereas previous sections of this report have explored changing patterns of drug use from the first relevant BCS survey in 1994, this chapter concentrates primarily on changes between 1998 and 2000. This is because 1998 is the baseline year for the anti-drugs strategy – the starting point adopted by Government for tracking changes in drug use by young people. Similarly, while earlier chapters have categorised young people in terms of different age groups, including both a broad definition (16–29) and various narrower ones, this chapter focuses on those aged 16–24, since this is a target age group for the anti-drugs strategy.

The targets set in the anti-drugs strategy are for reductions in the proportion of young people under 25 reporting use of illegal drugs in the previous year and last month. A more specific aim was to reduce last year and last month heroin and cocaine use in this age group by 25 per cent by 2005 and by 50 per cent by 2008, as set out by the United Kingdom Anti-Drugs Co-ordination Unit (UKADCU, 2000). However, a more wide-ranging target of reducing Class A drug use among under 25s has superseded this (UKADCU, 2001). Class A drugs included in the BCS are heroin, cocaine, (unprescribed) Methadone, crack, ecstasy, LSD and magic mushrooms. Of these, the two most widely used are cocaine and ecstasy, for which there are now broadly comparable prevalence rates in England and Wales (rates of use for all drugs for 16- to 24-year-olds are set out in Table B.5 in Appendix B). Combined levels of consumption of cocaine and ecstasy go a long way to determining overall rates of Class A drug use, rather as rates of use for cannabis largely determine those for 'any drug'.

Baselines and targets

What are the targets and the 1998 baselines and what has happened to the prevalence rates in the two-year period since then? Table 5.1 shows figures for the Class A target alongside the previous targets concerning cocaine and heroin. Unsurprisingly, changes in drug use for the 16–24 age group from 1998 broadly mirror those for the wider 16–29 age group, as previously discussed. There has been no significant increase in cocaine, heroin or Class A drug use (yet, by the same token, no significant declines).

Table 5.1: *Baseline rates and targets for use of cocaine, heroin and Class A drugs among 16- to 24-year-olds, in percentages (to two decimal places)*

	1998 prevalence (baseline)	2000 prevalence	2005 target (reduction of 25% from 1998)	2008 target (reduction of 50% from 1998)
Cocaine				
Last year	3.08	4.94	2.31	1.54
Last month	0.83	1.79	0.62	0.41
Heroin				
Last year	0.30	0.80	0.22	0.15
Last month	0.27	0.32	0.20	0.13
Class A				
Last year	8.28	9.24	6.21	4.14
Last month	3.43	4.76	2.57	1.71

Note: None of the increases from 1998 to 2000 were statistically significant. While the percentage increase for some drugs seems relatively large (e.g. use of heroin in the last year rose by 171 per cent), this is because only a small number of people use this drug and hence, small increases in the absolute numbers reporting use will have a disproportionately large effect. (To give a simplified example, if, from a total sample of 100 people, 50 report use of cannabis one year and this rises to 51 in the next, the percentage increase is two per cent. However, if two people in the same sample report heroin use and this goes up by one person the following year, then this is a 50 per cent increase). Source: 1998 and 2000 BCS (weighted data).

The broader picture

It is probably helpful to consider Table 5.1 alongside the broader and longer-term picture, as set out in Table 5.2, which illustrates drug use among 16- to 24-year-olds across the four relevant sweeps of the BCS, since 1994. All seven of the Class A drugs in the BCS are presented in the table. The key findings from Table 5.2 are:

- A significant increase was found for use of cocaine in the last year between 1994 and 2000 (from 1% to 5%) and between 1996 and 2000 (again from 1% to 5%). Use of cocaine in the last month rose significantly from 1994 and 1996 to 2000 (from less than 0.5% to 2%). For lifetime use of cocaine, there were statistically significant increases from 1994 (3%), 1996 (4%) and 1998 (7%) to 2000 (10%).

- Crack use among 16- to 24-year-olds was low and rates for use in the last year rose only slightly from less than 0.5 per cent in 1994 to one per cent in 2000. The only significant rise occurred for lifetime rates (1% in 1994 to 2% in 2000).

- Use of heroin among 16 to 24s also remained low, with no significant changes in last year or last month rates of use. Lifetime rates of use stayed at one per cent for 1994, 1996 and 1998, and rose slightly to two per cent for 2000.

- Less than 0.5 per cent of 16- to 24-year-olds reported (unprescribed) Methadone use in the last year and last month, a figure similar to previous years. Lifetime use also remained low at around one per cent.

- A significant rise in use of ecstasy in the last month occurred between 1994 and 2000 (from 2% to 3%). Although lifetime rates also increased significantly from eight per cent in 1994 to 11 per cent in 2000, they remained stable from 1996 onwards.

- Last year and last month use of LSD declined since 1994 (significantly in relation to last month use only). Lifetime use remained stable and was 11 per cent in 2000.

- No significant changes occurred for use of magic mushrooms, with last year and last month use at two per cent and one per cent respectively.

- Similarly, no significant changes occurred for use of cannabis in the last year and last month (26% and 17% respectively for 2000). However, lifetime use of cannabis rose significantly from 36 per cent in 1994 to 45 per cent in 2000. A significant increase also occurred between 1996 and 2000 (39% to 45%), but not between 1998 and 2000.

- Use of Class A drugs remained fairly stable across the years, with only slight (and non-significant) increases in use within the last year (from 8% in 1998 to 9% in 2000) and the last month (from 3% in 1998 to 5% in 2000). Lifetime use remained stable at around 20 per cent.

- Use of any drug in the last year, remained remarkably stable at 29 per cent for each of the four sweeps. Although use in the last month rose slightly from 17 per cent in 1994 to 18 per cent in 2000, no significant changes were found between any of the years. Lifetime drug use rose significantly from 45 per cent in 1994 to 50 per cent in 2000. However, lifetime rates of use, which could merely reflect one-off experimentation, among other factors, are not within the scope of the anti-drugs strategy targets.

Table 5.2: *Percentage of respondents aged 16 to 24 using various drugs in their lifetime, the last year and the last month, 1994 to 2000*

	1994	1996	1998	2000
Cocaine				
Lifetime	**3	**4	*7	10
Last year	**1	**1	3	5
Last month	*-	**-	1	2
Crack				
Lifetime	**1	2	2	2
Last year	-	-	-	1
Last month	0	-	-	-
Heroin				
Lifetime	1	1	1	2
Last year	1	-	-	1
Last month	-	-	-	-
Methadone				
Lifetime	1	-	1	1
Last year	1	-	1	-
Last month	-	-	-	-
Ecstasy				
Lifetime	*8	11	11	11
Last year	4	6	5	5
Last month	*2	3	2	3
LSD				
Lifetime	12	12	12	11
Last year	6	4	3	2
Last month	*2	1	-	1
Mushrooms				
Lifetime	11	9	11	10
Last year	4	2	4	2
Last month	-	-	-	1
Cannabis				
Lifetime	**36	*39	44	45
Last year	26	26	27	26
Last month	16	16	17	17

Class A				
Lifetime	20	19	20	20
Last year	9	9	8	9
Last month	3	4	3	5
Any drug				
Lifetime	*45	47	52	50
Last year	29	29	29	29
Last month	17	18	19	18

Note: Sample sizes for the 16 to 24 age group were 1,442 in 1994; 1,475 in 1996; 1,296 in 1998 and 1,517 in 2000. * = Significantly different from 2000 at $p<0.05$; ** = significantly different from 2000 at $p<0.01$. '-' indicates less than 0.5%. Source: 1994, 1996, 1998 and 2000 BCS (weighted data).

Focusing only on the period from 1998 to 2000, overall drug use remained fairly stable, as did use of cannabis. In addition, there were only very slight increases in use of heroin (last year), ecstasy (last month) and Class A (last year and last month). There was, however, a rise in cocaine use among 16- to 24-year-olds between 1998 and 2000. Because the increase is significant only for lifetime use of cocaine, this would suggest that more young people are trying the drug but perhaps not becoming monthly users.

Conclusion

What implications do these figures have for the future, given that the teenagers of today will determine the level of success of the anti-drugs strategy come 2005 and 2008? There may be grounds for guarded optimism, given the significant declines in use within the last year of any drug, amphetamine, LSD and poppers by 16- to 19-year-olds in 2000 compared with 1994. On the other hand, Chapter 3 reports significant increases in cocaine use among the 16- to 19-year-old age group, suggesting that some young people may be turning to cocaine instead of drugs such as ecstasy and amphetamine.

Urgent action to reduce drug use among young people is being undertaken by a range of Government departments. The Department for Education and Skills will be ensuring the delivery of statutory drug education in schools and supporting schools in developing drug education programmes. The Department of Health will be working with Health Authorities, Primary Care Trusts and Social Services Departments with the aim of routinely commissioning primary prevention activity for the general population and primary and secondary prevention activity for young people more at risk. The Home Office Drugs Prevention Advisory Service will be working with Drug Action Teams to develop the drug education element of their action plans. Specific initiatives include the National Healthy Schools Standard, launched in Autumn 1999 to encourage local schemes to promote healthy schools, and the ConneXions Service, which aims to provide each 13 to 19 year old with a personal adviser to assist in careers and academic planning and overcome personal and social problems. These personal advisers will also be responsible for identifying young people with problem drug use and for helping them to gain access to treatment and other assistance.

Population estimates

Finally, leaving aside the percentage prevalence rates, just how many young people are in the target group on which the Government is concentrating its attention? Table B.11 in Appendix B provides estimates of the number of 16- to 24-year-olds who consumed any drug, cannabis, heroin, cocaine and any Class A drug in the last year and last month, using data from the 2000 BCS. The upper and lower ranges, based on 95 per cent confidence intervals, are also included.

Equivalent information is also presented graphically for cocaine, heroin and Class A drugs in Figures 5.1 to 5.6. Of the 5.7 million young people aged 16 to 24 in England and Wales, at least 1.6 million used a prohibited drug in the last year and just over one million in the last month. However, most of them only consumed cannabis, for which the estimates were almost as high, at approximately 1.5 million for use in the last year and almost one million for use in the last month.

Figures 5.1 to 5.6 illustrate estimates for cocaine, heroin and Class A drug use for the four relevant sweeps of the BCS. Cocaine and heroin estimates are considerably lower than for other drugs, at 285,000 and 46,000 for the number of users in the last year respectively (for 2000). The 2000 BCS figures indicate that the estimated numbers of 16- to 24-year-olds who have used Class A drugs are roughly half a million on a last year basis and approximately quarter of a million for the last month.

As discussed earlier in this chapter, some of the changes from 1998 to 2000 in the proportion of 16- to 24-year-olds using certain drugs were rather large for some drugs, yet were not found to be statistically significant due to the small numbers involved (cf. Gore, 1999). From 2001, the BCS will be carried out every year, with a substantially larger sample, including a booster sample of 16- to 24-year-olds and some additional questions on access to and age of first use of Class A drugs. All of this will help to ensure more effective monitoring of the Government's ten-year strategy for tackling drug misuse.

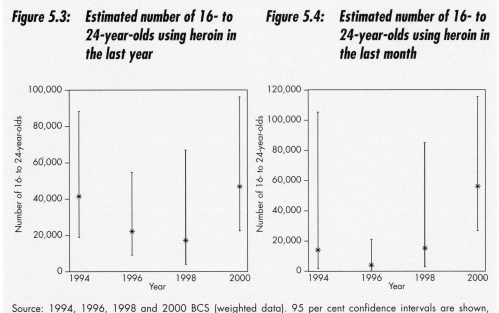

Figure 5.1: *Estimated number of 16- to 24-year-olds using cocaine in the last year*

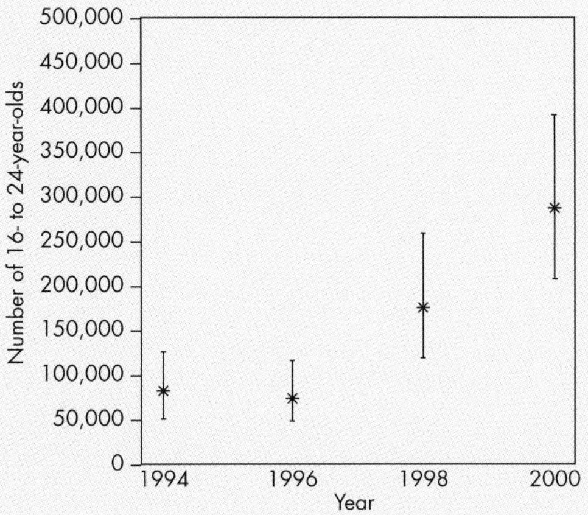

Figure 5.2: *Estimated number of 16- to 24-year-olds using cocaine in the last month*

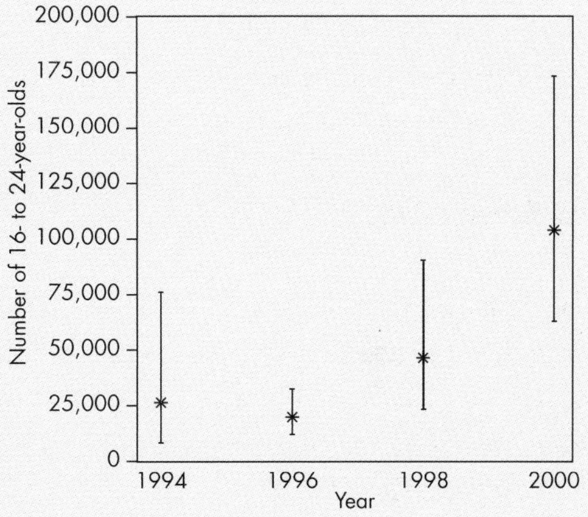

Source: 1994, 1996, 1998 and 2000 BCS (weighted data). 95 per cent confidence intervals are shown, calculated using logit transformations and relevant design effects.

Figure 5.3: *Estimated number of 16- to 24-year-olds using heroin in the last year*

Figure 5.4: *Estimated number of 16- to 24-year-olds using heroin in the last month*

Source: 1994, 1996, 1998 and 2000 BCS (weighted data). 95 per cent confidence intervals are shown, calculated using logit transformations and relevant design effects.

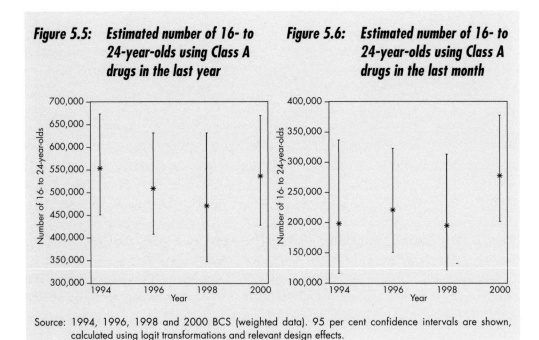

Figure 5.5: *Estimated number of 16- to 24-year-olds using Class A drugs in the last year*

Figure 5.6: *Estimated number of 16- to 24-year-olds using Class A drugs in the last month*

Source: 1994, 1996, 1998 and 2000 BCS (weighted data). 95 per cent confidence intervals are shown, calculated using logit transformations and relevant design effects.

Appendix A   Response rate and survey details

The BCS has been conducted every two years, the last survey being done in 1998, with continuous, annual sampling beginning in 2001. The 2000 BCS was the eighth sweep of the survey and interviews were conducted with a core sample of nearly 20,000 people resident in households in England and Wales. The survey was carried out in early 2000, with the bulk of interviews conducted between January and April, by the National Centre for Social Research and the Social Survey Division of the Office for National Statistics.

This survey differed from the 1998 BCS survey in that it also included an ethnic minority booster sample of around 4,000 people. (See Appendix C for further details on participation rates in the booster sample.) The information presented in this appendix only covers the core sample, in which there were some ethnic minority respondents; the booster is not included with one exception, Table A.19.

The drugs component of the 2000 BCS was conducted using a self-completion questionnaire, with the respondent entering their answers into a laptop computer. Respondents aged between 16 and 59 were eligible for the self-completion part of the survey. The questions and the format for the drugs module can be found in Appendix F. More detailed information on the survey can be found in the technical report for the 2000 BCS (Hales *et al.*, 2000).

Response rate for the BCS

At the 26,291 addresses obtained, 19,411 interviews were achieved, giving a response rate of 73.8 per cent. This is lower than the two previous sweeps (82.5% in 1996 and 78.7% in 1998).

Table A.1 below shows the degree of under-representation of 16- to 24-year-olds across the last three sweeps of the survey. It shows that young people are generally under-represented in the BCS sample, even after weighting has been applied, albeit at a consistent level. Under-representation may be due in part to lower response rates for this age group.

Table A.1: Under-representation of 16- to 24-year-olds, 1996 to 2000

	1996	1998	2000
Percentage of 16- to 24-year-olds in sample (unweighted)	9.2	8.9	8.0
Percentage of 16- to 24-year-olds in sample (weighted)	12.5	11.9	11.6
Estimated percentage of 16 to 24 year olds in the population	14.3	13.7	13.5
Degree of under-representation (proportion in in weighted sample – proportion in population)	-1.8	-1.8	-1.9

Note   The 1994 BCS technical report (White and Malbon, 1995) only records details for 16- to 29-year-olds; the
relevant figures were: percentage in sample (weighted) = 22 per cent; population estimate = 26 per cent.

Participation in the drugs component

13,300 people aged between 16 and 59 were asked to take part in the self-completion drugs component of the 2000 BCS survey. Of these, 279 (2.1%) refused, leaving a sample of 13,021 respondents.

Of the 13,021 participants, 829 (6.2%) needed help from the interviewer to complete the questions, a slightly higher rate than for the 1998 survey. Table A.2 shows the participation rates for the 1994, 1996, 1998 and 2000 surveys.

Table A.2: Participation rates for 1994, 1996, 1998 and 2000 BCS drugs components

	1994	%	1996	%	1998	%	2000	%
Refused to participate	241	2.4	304	2.7	305	3.0	279	2.1
Self-completion	8,753	88.5	10,389	92.4	9,529	92.6	12,192	91.7
Assisted self-completion	893	9.0	551	4.9	459	4.5	829	6.2
Total (contact sample)	9,889	100	11,244	100	10,293	100	13,300	100
Of which: all participants, respondent and assisted	9,646	97.5	10,940	97.3	9,988	97.0	13,021	97.9

It is not possible to say whether all respondents who took part in the self-completion drugs questions answered truthfully. The data obtained probably underestimate the prevalence of drug use in the population. In addition, respondents were given another option (apart from 'yes' or 'no') when asked if they had taken a particular drug. They could have chosen 'don't want to answer', which could sometimes conceivably imply 'yes'. However, there is no way of being sure about this and, as in previous reports, the analysis of the data has assumed that 'don't want to answer' means 'no'. This conservative approach means that only those who definitively declare their drug use are taken into consideration.

Sample sizes

The unweighted sample sizes for the various age groups of respondents explored in the analyses in this report are displayed in the following tables for the 2000, 1998, 1996 and 1994 BCS.

Table A.3: Sample sizes in the 2000 BCS drugs component by age group

Age	Men	Women	Total
16–19	302	363	665
20–24	394	458	852
25–29	671	827	1,498
30–34	865	1,031	1,896
35–39	858	1,024	1,882
40–44	770	893	1,663
45–59	2,204	2,361	4,565
16–59	6,064	6,957	13,021

Table A.4: Sample sizes in the 1998 BCS drugs component by age group

Age	Men	Women	Total
16–19	248	254	502
20–24	284	510	794
25–29	495	749	1,244
30–34	677	898	1,575
35–39	645	795	1,440
40–44	573	668	1,241
45–59	1,494	1,698	3,192
16–59	4,416	5,572	9,988

Table A.5: Sample sizes in the 1996 BCS drugs component by age group

Age	Men	Women	Total
16–19	308	273	581
20–24	362	532	894
25–29	664	887	1,551
30–34	749	949	1,698
35–39	689	796	1,485
40–44	602	639	1,241
45–59	1,654	1,836	3,490
16–59	5,028	5,912	10,940

Table A.6: Sample sizes in the 1994 BCS drugs component by age group

Age	Men	Women	Total
16–19	248	290	538
20–24	380	524	904
25–29	576	759	1,335
30–34	662	890	1,552
35–39	621	708	1,329
40–44	517	560	1,077
45–59	1,442	1,469	2,911
16–59	4,446	5,200	9,646

Table A.7: Sample sizes for 16- to 29-year-olds by region, 1994 to 2000

	London	Anglia	North	South	Midlands	Wales	England & Wales
1994	403	112	900	708	498	156	2,777
1996	491	145	882	838	515	155	3,026
1998	443	101	738	642	468	148	2,540
2000	405	142	896	775	568	229	3,015

Table A.8: *Sample sizes for 16- to 29-year-olds by ACORN category, 1994 to 2000*

	Affluent suburban/ rural	Affluent family	Affluent urban	Mature home-owning	New home-owning	Council estates/ low income	All
1994	303	277	280	664	396	857	2,777
1996	392	310	343	662	430	886	3,023
1998	270	300	302	564	315	784	2,535
2000	392	380	299	783	449	706	3,009

Table A.9: *Sample sizes by income and age group, 2000*

	16–29	30–59	All
Poorest (<£5,000)	295	674	969
Intermediate (£5,000–£29,999)	1,600	5,762	7,362
Richest (£30,000+)	761	3,136	3,897

Table A.10: *Sample sizes by educational attainment and age group, 2000*

	16–19	20–24	25–29	30–59	All
No qualifications	150	101	204	2,559	3,014
Intermediate	512	621	955	5,627	7,715
Degree	3	128	338	1,814	2,283

Table A.11: *Sample sizes by social class, 2000*

	16–29	30–59	All
Lowest	147	410	557
Intermediate	1,748	4,980	6,728
Top two	614	3,190	3,804

Table A.12: Sample sizes for 16- to 29-year-olds by employment status, 1994 to 2000

	Working	Unemployed	Economically inactive	All
1994	1,716	282	779	2,777
1996	1,937	221	866	3,024
1998	1,637	147	750	2,534
2000	2,100	179	735	3,014

Table A.13: Sample sizes for housing tenure by age group, 2000

	16–29	30–59	Total
Owners	1,403	7,735	9,138
Social Rented	580	1,455	2,035
Private Rented	875	749	1,624
All	2,858	9,939	12,797

Table A.14: Sample sizes for marital status by age group, 2000

	16–29	30–59	Total
Single	2,326	1,765	4,091
Married/ Cohabiting	583	6,075	6,658
Separated/ Divorced	105	1,919	2,024
Widowed	1	242	243
All	3,015	10,001	13,016

Table A.15: Sample sizes for visits to the pub in the evening by age group, 2000

	16–29	30–59	Total
Less than 3 times a week	2,480	9,208	11,688
3 or more times a week	535	797	1,332
All	3,015	10,005	13,020

Table A.16:   Sample sizes for alcohol consumption by age group, 2000

	16–29	30–59	Total
3 or more days a week	734	3,279	4,013
1 to 2 days a week	1,052	3,080	4,132
2 to 3 times a month or less	1,229	3,639	4,868
All	3,015	9,998	13,013

Table A.17:   Sample sizes for nightclub visits by age group, 2000

	16–29	30–59	Total
Less than once a week	2,645	9,866	12,511
At least once a week	370	139	509
All	3,015	10,005	13,020

Table A.18:   Sample sizes for general health status by age group, 2000

	16–29	30–59	Total
Very good	1,422	4,268	5,690
Good	1,158	3,680	4,838
Fair	380	1,650	2,030
Bad	55	404	459
All	3,015	10,002	13,017

Table A.19:   Sample sizes for ethnic groups, 2000 (core and boost)

	16–29	30–59	Total
White	2,742	9,430	12,172
Black – Caribbean	162	582	744
Black – African	156	357	513
Black – other	66	111	177
Indian	337	818	1,155
Pakistani	277	306	583
Bangladeshi	94	100	194
Chinese	15	35	50
Mixed	106	135	241
None of these	59	192	251
All	4,014	12,066	16,080

Table B.1: *Percentage of respondents who said they had heard of drugs, 1998 and 2000*

	16–29		30–59		16–59	
	1998	2000	1998	2000	1998	2000
Cocaine	98	98	99	99	99	99
Cannabis	98	98	98	98	98	98
Ecstasy	98	98	98	98	98	98
Heroin	97	98	98	98	98	98
LSD	96	96	97	97	97	97
Valium, Temazepam	94	93	96	97	96	96
Crack	93	95	93	94	93	95
Steroids	93	93	95	95	94	94
Amphetamine	94	93	92	92	93	92
Magic mushrooms	92	93	86	88	87	89
Methadone	77	83	82	88	81	87
Poppers	75	75	66	68	68	70
Semeron	7	8	4	4	4	5

Note: Details of sample sizes for this and following tables can be found in Appendix A. Source: 1998 and 2000 BCS (weighted data). Semeron is a bogus substance.

Table B.2: Percentage of men and women in the 2000 BCS who indicated that they had ever taken particular drugs, by age group

	16–19	20–24	25–29	30–34	35–39	40–44	45–59	All 16–59	All 16–29
Cannabis									
Men	40	55	52	46	36	28	17	33	50
Women	34	49	34	27	20	19	9	22	38
All	37	52	43	36	27	23	13	27	44
Amphetamine									
Men	15	27	30	21	12	8	5	14	25
Women	12	28	16	11	7	7	3	9	18
All	13	28	23	16	10	8	4	11	22
LSD									
Men	8	17	17	11	6	5	3	8	14
Women	6	13	6	4	2	3	1	4	8
All	7	15	12	8	4	4	2	6	11
Magic mushrooms									
Men	6	18	18	17	10	6	3	9	15
Women	4	10	6	8	4	4	1	4	7
All	5	14	12	12	7	5	2	6	11
Smoke unknown									
Men	8	8	10	6	5	5	3	5	9
Women	7	6	4	3	3	2	2	3	6
All	8	7	7	4	4	3	2	4	7
Ecstasy									
Men	9	19	19	10	3	2	-	6	16
Women	5	12	9	5	1	1	1	3	9
All	7	15	14	7	2	1	-	5	12
Temazepam, etc.									
Men	2	10	6	3	2	2	3	4	6
Women	3	2	4	3	3	4	4	4	3
All	2	6	5	3	3	3	4	4	5
Glue, etc.									
Men	6	9	6	7	2	1	1	3	7
Women	8	6	3	3	-	-	-	2	5
All	7	7	4	5	1	1	-	3	6
Cocaine									
Men	8	16	17	9	4	4	2	7	14
Women	4	11	5	5	2	3	1	3	7
All	6	14	11	7	3	3	1	5	10

Pills									
Men	3	4	5	2	1	1	1	2	4
Women	2	3	2	1	1	1	1	1	2
All	3	3	4	1	1	1	1	2	3
Crack									
Men	2	3	3	2	1	-	-	1	3
Women	1	2	1	1	1	-	-	1	1
All	2	2	2	1	1	-	-	1	2
Methadone									
Men	-	2	2	1	-	-	-	1	1
Women	0	-	-	-	-	-	-	-	-
All	-	1	1	1	-	-	-	-	1
Heroin									
Men	1	3	3	3	1	1	-	1	2
Women	1	2	1	1	-	1	-	1	1
All	1	2	2	2	1	1	-	1	2
Poppers									
Men	9	23	23	16	7	5	2	9	19
Women	12	16	11	7	2	1	1	5	13
All	11	19	17	12	5	3	1	7	16
Steroids									
Men	1	2	3	2	2	1	1	1	2
Women	-	-	1	1	-	1	1	1	-
All	-	1	2	1	1	1	1	1	1
Semeron									
Men	0	0	0	0	0	0	0	0	0
Women	0	0	0	-	0	0	-	-	0
All	0	0	0	-	0	0	-	-	0
Anything else									
Men	2	4	3	1	2	1	1	2	3
Women	2	1	1	-	-	-	-	1	1
All	2	3	2	1	1	-	-	1	2
Any drug									
Men	44	63	60	54	43	35	23	40	56
Women	40	54	40	33	26	24	15	28	44
All	42	58	50	43	34	29	19	34	50

Note: '-' indicates less than 0.5% (this convention is used in the rest of the tables in this Appendix). Source:2000
BCS (weighted data).   Semeron is a bogus substance.

Table B.3: Percentage of men and women in the 2000 BCS who indicated that they had taken particular drugs in the last year, by age group

	16–19	20–24	25–29	30–34	35–39	40–44	45–59	All 16–59	All 16–29
Cannabis									
Men	28	30	23	15	9	6	3	12	27
Women	21	24	12	6	4	3	1	7	18
All	25	27	17	10	6	4	2	9	22
Amphetamine									
Men	8	6	7	3	1	-	-	3	7
Women	4	6	1	2	-	-	-	1	3
All	6	6	4	2	1	-	-	2	5
LSD									
Men	4	4	2	1	-	-	-	1	3
Women	1	1	-	-	0	0	-	-	1
All	2	2	1	-	-	-	-	1	2
Magic mushrooms									
Men	4	4	2	1	-	-	-	1	3
Women	1	1	-	-	-	0	-	-	-
All	2	2	1	-	-	-	-	1	2
Smoke unknown									
Men	2	1	1	1	-	-	-	1	2
Women	2	-	-	-	-	0	-	-	1
All	2	1	1	-	-	-	-	1	1
Ecstasy									
Men	6	8	8	2	-	-	-	2	7
Women	4	3	1	1	-	0	-	1	3
All	5	6	4	2	-	-	-	2	5
Temazepam, etc.									
Men	1	3	1	-	-	-	-	1	2
Women	1	1	1	-	-	1	-	1	1
All	1	2	1	-	-	1	-	1	1
Glue, etc.									
Men	2	-	-	0	-	-	0	-	1
Women	2	-	0	0	0	0	-	-	1
All	2	-	-	0	-	-	-	-	1
Cocaine									
Men	6	8	8	3	1	1	-	3	7
Women	2	4	2	1	-	-	-	1	3
All	4	6	5	2	-	-	-	2	5

Pills									
Men	-	1	-	-	-	0	-	-	-
Women	1	0	-	-	-	0	-	-	-
All	-	-	-	-	-	0	-	-	-
Crack									
Men	1	2	1	1	0	-	-	1	1
Women	-	-	-	-	-	0	-	-	-
All	1	1	1	1	-	-	-	-	1
Methadone									
Men	-	-	-	-	-	0	0	-	-
Women	0	0	0	0	0	0	-	-	0
All	-	-	-	-	-	0	-	-	-
Heroin									
Men	1	2	1	1	-	-	0	-	1
Women	1	-	-	0	-	0	-	-	-
All	1	1	1	-	-	-	-	-	1
Poppers									
Men	5	5	4	2	1	-	-	2	4
Women	3	4	-	1	-	-	-	1	2
All	4	4	2	1	-	-	-	1	3
Steroids									
Men	-	-	1	-	0	0	-	-	-
Women	0	0	-	-	0	-	-	-	-
All	-	-	-	-	0	-	-	-	-
Semeron									
Men	0	0	0	0	0	0	0	0	0
Women	0	0	0	0	0	0	-	-	0
All	0	0	0	0	0	0	-	-	0
Anything else									
Men	1	-	-	-	0	0	0	-	1
Women	0	-	-	-	-	0	-	-	-
All	-	-	-	-	-	0	-	-	-
Any drug									
Men	31	34	26	17	10	7	4	14	30
Women	24	26	14	7	4	3	2	8	20
All	27	30	20	12	7	5	3	11	25

Source: 2000 BCS (weighted data). Semeron is a bogus substance.

Table B.4: Percentage of men and women in the 2000 BCS who indicated that they had taken particular drugs in the last month, by age group

	16–19	20–24	25–29	30–34	35–39	40–44	45–59	All 16–59	All 16–29
Cannabis									
Men	20	21	17	9	5	4	2	8	19
Women	11	15	6	3	1	1	-	4	10
All	15	18	11	6	3	3	1	6	14
Amphetamine									
Men	5	2	3	1	1	-	-	1	3
Women	2	3	1	1	-	-	-	1	2
All	3	3	2	1	-	-	-	1	2
LSD									
Men	1	1	0	-	0	-	0	-	1
Women	-	-	0	-	0	0	-	-	-
All	1	1	0	-	0	-	-	-	-
Magic mushrooms									
Men	2	1	1	-	0	-	-	-	1
Women	-	0	-	-	-	0	-	-	-
All	1	1	-	-	-	-	-	-	1
Smoke unknown									
Men	1	-	-	-	-	-	-	-	1
Women	-	-	-	-	-	0	-	-	-
All	1	-	-	-	-	-	-	-	-
Ecstasy									
Men	6	4	4	1	-	-	0	1	4
Women	1	2	-	-	-	0	-	-	1
All	3	3	2	1	-	-	-	1	3
Temazepam, etc.									
Men	0	1	-	-	-	-	-	-	-
Women	0	-	-	0	0	1	-	-	-
All	0	1	-	-	-	-	-	-	-
Glue, etc.									
Men	1	0	0	0	0	-	0	-	-
Women	-	-	0	0	0	0	-	-	-
All	1	-	0	0	0	-	-	-	-
Cocaine									
Men	3	2	4	1	-	-	-	1	3
Women	1	-	-	-	-	0	-	-	1
All	2	1	2	1	-	-	-	1	2

Pills									
Men	-	-	0	0	0	0	-	-	-
Women	-	0	0	-	-	0	0	-	-
All	-	-	0	-	-	0	-	-	-
Crack									
Men	-	-	1	-	0	-	0	-	-
Women	-	-	0	-	0	0	-	-	-
All	-	-	-	-	0	-	-	-	-
Methadone									
Men	0	-	0	-	-	0	0	-	-
Women	0	0	0	0	0	0	-	-	0
All	0	-	0	-	-	0	-	-	-
Heroin									
Men	-	1	1	-	-	-	0	-	1
Women	-	0	0	0	-	0	-	-	-
All	-	-	-	-	-	-	-	-	-
Poppers									
Men	3	2	2	-	-	0	-	1	2
Women	1	2	-	-	0	0	0	-	1
All	2	2	1	-	-	0	-	1	2
Steroids									
Men	-	0	-	0	0	0	-	-	-
Women	0	0	-	0	0	-	-	-	-
All	-	0	-	0	0	-	-	-	-
Semeron									
Men	0	0	0	0	0	0	0	0	0
Women	0	0	0	0	0	0	0	0	0
All	0	0	0	0	0	0	0	0	0
Anything else									
Men	0	0	0	-	0	0	0	-	0
Women	0	0	0	-	0	0	-	-	0
All	0	0	0	-	0	0	-	-	0
Any drug									
Men	21	23	19	9	5	5	2	9	21
Women	12	16	6	4	2	2	1	4	11
All	16	20	12	6	3	3	2	6	16

Source: 2000 BCS (weighted data). Semeron is a bogus substance.

Table B.5: *Percentage of men and women in the 16 to 24 age group who indicated that they had taken particular drugs in their lifetime, the last year and the last month, 2000*

	Lifetime	Last year	Last month
Cannabis			
Men	48	29	21
Women	41	23	13
All	45	26	17
Amphetamine			
Men	21	7	3
Women	20	5	3
All	21	6	3
LSD			
Men	13	4	1
Women	10	1	-
All	11	2	1
Magic mushrooms			
Men	13	4	1
Women	7	1	-
All	10	2	1
Smoke unknown			
Men	8	2	1
Women	7	1	-
All	7	2	1
Ecstasy			
Men	14	7	5
Women	9	4	2
All	11	5	3
Temazepam, etc.			
Men	6	2	1
Women	3	1	-
All	4	1	-
Glue, etc.			
Men	7	1	-
Women	7	1	-
All	7	1	-
Cocaine			
Men	12	7	3
Women	8	3	1
All	10	5	2

Pills			
Men	4	1	-
Women	3	-	-
All	3	-	-
Crack			
Men	2	1	-
Women	2	-	-
All	2	1	-
Methadone			
Men	1	-	-
Women	-	0	0
All	1	-	-
Heroin			
Men	2	1	-
Women	1	-	-
All	2	1	-
Poppers			
Men	17	5	2
Women	14	3	1
All	15	4	2
Steroids			
Men	2	-	-
Women	-	0	0
All	1	-	-
Semeron			
Men	0	0	0
Women	0	0	0
All	0	0	0
Anything else			
Men	3	1	0
Women	2	-	0
All	2	-	0
Any drug			
Men	54	33	22
Women	47	25	14
All	50	29	18

Source: 2000 BCS (weighted data). Semeron is a bogus drug.

Table B.6: *Percentage of respondents aged 16 to 29 using various drugs in the last year and the last month by Government Office Region, 2000*

	Cocaine		Heroin		Any drug		Hallucinants		Class A	
	Yr	Mth	Yr	Mth	Yr	Mth	Yr	Mth	Yr	Mth
London	12	4	-	-	31	22	11	6	14	6
North West	5	3	-	0	30	18	11	6	8	5
South East	5	3	1	-	27	17	7	4	6	4
Yorks. & Humbs.	2	-	1	1	24	12	13	4	10	3
East Midlands	4	-	2	-	23	13	9	3	7	2
Eastern	3	2	1	0	23	15	6	4	5	4
South West	6	2	1	0	22	14	9	5	9	5
North East	4	3	2	2	21	15	13	8	9	5
West Midlands	2	-	-	-	20	11	6	3	5	2
Wales	3	0	0	0	19	13	6	5	5	2
England & Wales	5	2	1	-	25	16	9	5	8	4

Note: There is a slight difference in how Government Office Regions and Standard Regions are defined. As a result, some of the percentages for certain regions (e.g. London) may differ across the regional classifications. Source: 2000 BCS (weighted data). 'Yr' = in the last year; 'Mth' = in the last month.

Table B.7: *Percentage of respondents using any drug in the last year by ACORN category and age group, 2000*

	16–29	30–59	All
Affluent suburban and rural areas	21	3	7
Affluent family areas	20	4	7
Affluent urban areas	40	15	25
Mature home-owning areas	24	5	10
New home-owning areas	25	6	11
Council estates and low income areas	23	7	13

Source: 2000 BCS (weighted data).

Table B.8: *Percentage of respondents aged 16 to 29 using various drugs in the last year by ACORN category, 2000*

	Cocaine	Crack	Heroin	Any drug	Halluci- nants	Class A
Affluent suburban and rural areas	5	1	0	21	6	6
Affluent family areas	3	1	1	20	4	4
Affluent urban areas	11	0	-	40	15	16
Mature home-owning areas	4	1	1	24	9	8
New home-owning areas	5	1	-	25	9	8
Council estates and low income areas	4	1	1	23	9	8

Source: 2000 BCS (weighted data).

Table B.9: *Percentage of respondents using any drug in the last year by household tenure and age group, 2000*

	16–29	30–59	All
Owners/part-owners	19	5	7
Social rented sector	23	7	12
Private rented sector	33	11	25
All	25	5	10

Note: In the 16–29 age group: 45% owners/part-owners; 15% social rented; 34% private rented. In the 30-59 age group: 79% owners/part-owners; 13% social rented; 7% private rented. Source: 2000 BCS (weighted data). The overall percentage is 10% rather than 11% because of missing values.

Table B.10: *Percentage of respondents using any drug in the last year by marital status and age group, 2000*

	16–29	30–59	All
Single	28	13	23
Married/cohabiting	11	3	4
Separated/divorced	22	9	9
Widowed	See note	4	4
All	25	5	11

Note: In the 16–29 age group: 81% single; 17% married/cohabiting; 2% separated/divorced; less than 1% widowed. In the 30–59 age group: 14% single; 70% married/cohabiting; 14% separated/divorced; 2% widowed. Only one 16- to 29-year-old was widowed. Source: 2000 BCS (weighted data).

Table B.11: **Estimates of the number of 16- to 24-year-olds using various drugs in the last year and the last month in England and Wales, 2000**

	Best estimate	Lower estimate	Higher estimate
Cocaine			
Number using in the last year	285,000	207,000	390,000
Number using in the last month	103,000	62,000	172,000
Crack			
Number using in the last year	50,000	23,000	107,000
Number using in the last month	11,000	2,000	53,000
Heroin			
Number using in the last year	46,000	22,000	95,000
Number using in the last month	18,000	6,000	60,000
Cannabis			
Number using in the last year	1,503,000	1,308,000	1,698,000
Number using in the last month	959,000	823,000	1,113,000
Any drug			
Number using in the last year	1,649,000	1,449,000	1,848,000
Number using in the last month	1,036,000	894,000	1,195,000
Class A			
Number using in the last year	533,000	425,000	666,000
Number using in the last month	275,000	201,000	374,000

Note: Source 2000 BCS (weighted data), together with ONS 1999 mid-year population estimates. The upper and lower estimates encompass the 95% confidence range (calculated using a logit transformation for those proportions that were less than 0.2 [or greater than 0.8] to ensure that lower estimates did not fall below zero) together with varying design effects for different drugs. The estimated number of 16- to 24-year-olds in England and Wales in 2000 is 5,768,000. Figures have been rounded to the nearest 1,000.

Appendix C

Minority ethnic booster sample

Table C.1: *Percentage of respondents using various drugs in their lifetime by age and ethnic group, 2000*

	White	All black groups	Indian	Pakistani/ Bangladeshi
Cannabis				
16–29	46	32	21	9
30–59	22	20	4	2
All, 16–59	28	24	10	6
Amphetamine				
16–29	23	6	6	2
30–59	8	4	1	1
All, 16–59	12	5	3	1
LSD				
16–29	12	2	3	2
30–59	4	2	-	-
All, 16–59	6	2	1	1
Magic mushrooms				
16–29	10	1	4	1
30–59	5	2	-	-
All, 16–59	7	2	2	1
Smoke unknown				
16–29	7	6	4	4
30–59	3	3	1	2
All, 16–59	4	4	2	3
Ecstasy				
16–29	12	5	7	2
30–59	2	2	-	-
All, 16–59	5	3	2	1
Temazepam, etc.				
16–29	5	2	1	1
30–59	3	2	2	2
All, 16–59	4	2	1	1
Glue, etc.				
16–29	6	1	1	1
30–59	1	1	-	1
All, 16–59	3	1	1	1

Cocaine				
16–29	10	6	7	1
30–59	3	2	1	1
All, 16–59	5	3	3	1
Pills unknown				
16–29	3	3	2	2
30–59	1	1	1	0
All, 16–59	2	1	1	1
Crack				
16–29	2	3	2	-
30–59	1	1	-	0
All, 16–59	1	1	1	-
Methadone				
16–29	1	-	-	0
30–59	-	1	0	0
All, 16–59	-	1	-	0
Heroin				
16–29	2	-	1	-
30–59	1	1	0	0
All, 16–59	1	1	-	-
Poppers				
16–29	17	3	3	1
30–59	4	2	-	0
All, 16–59	7	2	1	1
Steroids				
16–29	1	-	-	1
30–59	1	1	1	-
All, 16–59	1	1	1	1
Semeron				
16–29	0	0	0	0
30–59	-	-	0	0
All, 16–59	-	-	0	0
Anything else				
16–29	2	3	0	2
30–59	1	2	-	-
All, 16–59	1	2	-	1
Any drug				
16–29	52	37	25	13
30–59	28	24	9	8
All, 16–59	34	28	15	10

Note: '-' indicates less than 0.5% (this convention is used in the rest of the tables in this Appendix). Source: 2000 BCS core and booster samples (weighted data). Semeron is a bogus substance.

Table C.2: *Percentage of respondents who gave different 'Don't want to answer'*
(DWA) responses to 'lifetime' questions by age and ethnic group, 2000

	White	All black groups	Indian	Pakistani/ Bangladeshi
Cannabis				
16–29	2	3	3	2
30–59	1	1	1	0
All, 16–59	1	2	2	1
Amphetamine				
16–29	2	1	1	1
30–59	1	-	1	-
All, 16–59	1	1	1	1
LSD				
16–29	1	1	2	0
30–59	-	1	1	1
All, 16–59	1	1	1	1
Magic mushrooms				
16–29	1	1	1	0
30–59	-	1	2	0
All, 16–59	1	1	1	0
Smoke unknown				
16–29	1	-	2	1
30–59	-	1	1	-
All, 16–59	-	1	1	1
Ecstasy				
16–29	1	1	1	1
30–59	-	1	1	0
All, 16–59	1	1	1	1
Temazepam, etc.				
16–29	1	1	2	0
30–59	-	1	1	0
All, 16–59	-	1	1	0
Glue, etc.				
16–29	1	-	1	1
30–59	-	1	1	1
All, 16–59	-	1	1	1

Cocaine				
16–29	1	1	1	-
30–59	-	1	1	-
All, 16–59	1	1	1	-
Pills unknown				
16–29	1	1	1	1
30–59	-	1	1	-
All, 16–59	-	1	1	1
Crack				
16–29	1	1	2	1
30–59	-	1	1	1
All, 16–59	-	1	1	1
Methadone				
16–29	1	-	1	-
30–59	-	1	1	1
All, 16–59	-	1	1	-
Heroin				
16–29	1	1	1	1
30–59	-	-	1	0
All, 16–59	-	1	1	-
Poppers				
16–29	1	0	1	0
30–59	-	-	3	2
All, 16–59	1	-	2	1
Steroids				
16–29	1	-	1	-
30–59	-	1	1	1
All, 16–59	-	-	1	1
Semeron				
16–29	1	4	5	0
30–59	1	0	7	0
All, 16–59	1	1	6	0
Anything else				
16–29	1	1	1	1
30–59	-	1	1	-
All, 16–59	-	1	1	1

Source: 2000 BCS, core and booster samples (weighted data). Semeron is a bogus substance.

Table C.3 *Percentage of respondents reporting that they had taken cannabis in last year, or giving 'DWA' responses for cannabis (ever or last year questions), by age and ethnic group, 1994, 1996 and 2000*

	16–29			16–59		
	1994	1996	2000	1994	1996	2000
White						
Used cannabis, year	21	22	23	8	9	9
DWA cannabis, ever	2	2	2	1	1	1
DWA cannabis, year	-	1	1	-	-	1
All black groups						
Used cannabis, year	16	17	20	10	9	12
DWA cannabis, ever	4	4	3	2	2	2
DWA cannabis, year	0	0	1	0	0	1
Indian						
Used cannabis, year	5	8	10	3	4	4
DWA cannabis, ever	2	2	3	1	1	2
DWA cannabis, year	2	2	4	1	1	3
Pakistani/Bangladeshi						
Used cannabis, year	6	8	5	4	5	3
DWA cannabis, ever	1	2	2	-	1	1
DWA cannabis, year	0	0	2	0	0	2

Source: 2000 BCS, core and booster samples (weighted data).

Appendix D

Design effects

Table D.1: *Design effects for BCS drugs questions for 16- to 59-year-olds, 1994–2000*

	1994	1996	1998	2000
Amphetamine				
Ever	1.16	1.24	1.32	1.42
Last year	1.20	1.16	1.30	1.26
Last month	1.20	1.20	1.22	1.23
Cannabis				
Ever	1.35	1.30	1.39	1.41
Last year	1.26	1.27	1.48	1.53
Last month	-	1.31	1.38	1.34
Cocaine				
Ever	1.17	1.25	1.28	1.64
Last year	1.21	1.14	1.30	1.43
Last month	1.26	1.04	1.10	1.37
Crack				
Ever	1.06	1.24	1.24	1.23
Last year	0.81	1.23	1.13	1.42
Last month	0.83	1.36	1.03	1.38
Ecstasy				
Ever	1.17	1.37	1.21	1.36
Last year	1.17	1.21	1.31	1.36
Last month	1.22	1.15	1.17	1.38
Heroin				
Ever	1.16	1.15	1.22	1.23
Last year	1.48	1.06	1.38	1.30
Last month	1.67	0.96	1.64	1.34
LSD				
Ever	1.20	1.28	1.29	1.28
Last year	1.22	1.21	1.42	1.39
Last month	1.37	1.08	1.23	1.36
Methadone				
Ever	1.25	1.00	1.27	1.28
Last year	1.46	0.97	1.65	1.00
Last month	0.86	1.02	1.76	0.91

Mushrooms				
Ever	1.33	1.18	1.27	1.23
Last year	1.19	1.39	1.45	1.32
Last month	1.17	1.21	1.08	1.28
Other unknown				
Ever	1.07	1.17	1.06	1.26
Last year	1.19	1.00	0.98	1.12
Last month	1.13	1.00	1.03	0.88
Pills unknown				
Ever	1.19	1.29	1.23	1.19
Last year	1.24	1.14	1.32	1.09
Last month	1.07	1.00	1.01	1.11
Poppers				
Ever	1.28	1.21	1.22	1.35
Last year	1.25	1.27	1.23	1.35
Last month	1.23	1.16	1.20	1.33
Semeron				
Ever	0.76	0.87	-	1.10
Last year	0.76	0.68	-	1.02
Last month	0.76	0.74	-	-
Smoke unknown				
Ever	1.22	1.13	1.19	1.17
Last year	1.34	1.28	1.15	1.12
Last month	1.42	1.31	1.15	1.08
Solvents				
Ever	1.24	1.14	1.17	1.18
Last year	1.46	1.20	1.18	1.21
Last month	1.57	1.19	1.23	1.18
Steroids				
Ever	1.08	1.13	1.11	1.12
Last year	1.05	1.13	1.05	1.17
Last month	0.96	1.17	0.97	1.06
Tranquillisers				
Ever	1.21	1.06	1.09	1.25
Last year	1.06	1.05	1.19	1.20
Last month	1.13	1.01	1.29	1.14
Any drug				
Ever	1.36	1.31	1.38	1.40
Last year	1.30	1.28	1.45	1.52
Last month	1.26	1.28	1.36	1.35

Note: Only design effects (defts) for the full 16 to 59 age range were calculated for the 1998 and 2000 datasets and these were incorporated into all statistical tests involving these datasets. However, age-specific defts were used when these were available (for the 1994 and 1996 data). These additional defts can be obtained from the authors on request, see Appendix E. '-' = not available.

Appendix E

In this report, statistical tests were used to assess whether the differences between pairs of proportions were significant, either between various groups in the 2000 BCS or within the same groups across surveys. For example, the proportion of 16- to 19-year-olds who used any illicit drug in the last year fell from 34.1 per cent (p_1) in 1994 to 27.0 per cent in 2000 (p_2). In other words, the difference between the two proportions ($p_1 - p_2$) was 7.1 percentage points. The test below shows how the statistical significance of this difference was calculated (it was found to be significant at $p=0.036$, or, in other words, between 1 and 5 per cent). This implies that the change represented something other than normal sampling errors, i.e. that there was a 'real' decrease in drug-using behaviour among this age group.

Test of proportions

To test whether there was a statistically significant difference between these two groups at the 1 or 5 per cent level, one would calculate:

$$z = \frac{p_1 - p_2}{\sqrt{(d_1 se_2)^2 + (d_2 se_2)^2}} \qquad (1)$$

The first step being calculation of the respective standard errors (se) for the proportion of 16- to 19-year-olds using any drug in the last year in 1994 and 2000. The formula for this is:

$$se_1 = \sqrt{\frac{p_1(1-p_1)}{n_1}} \qquad (2)$$

where p_1 is the proportion of 16- to 19-year-olds using any drug in the last year in the 1994 BCS (0.340) and n_1 is the number of 16- to 19-year-olds asked the question (538). The same applies to the 2000 data, where $p_2 = 0.271$ and $n_2 = 665$.

The next step is to multiply these standard errors by their respective design effects (see paragraph below), summing the squares and taking the square root. This gives the standard error of the difference in the two proportions and dividing this into the difference in proportions (0.071) gives a z score to test for significance against standard normal tables. Two-tailed tests were used, so if the results were greater than 1.96, then that was judged significant at the five per cent level; results greater than or equal to 2.58 were significant at the one per cent level.

In the case above, the calculations were:

$$d_1se_1 \quad = \quad d_1\sqrt{\frac{p_1(1-p_1)}{n_1}}$$

$$= \quad 1.053\sqrt{\frac{0.341\,(1-0.341)}{538}}$$

$$= \quad 0.022$$

$$d_1se_2 \quad = \quad d_2\sqrt{\frac{p_2(1-p_2)}{n_2}}$$

$$= \quad 1.518\sqrt{\frac{0.271\,(1-0.271)}{665}}$$

$$= \quad 0.026$$

Then, to calculate the standard error of the difference (the denominator in equation (1) above),

$$= \quad \sqrt{(d_1se_2)^2+(d_2se_2)^2}$$

$$= \quad \sqrt{0.022^2+0.026^2}$$

$$= \quad 0.034$$

Finally,

$$z \quad = \quad \frac{0.341 - 0.270}{0.034}$$

$$= \quad 2.102$$

In statistical tables for the normal distribution, the two-tailed p value corresponding to z = 2.102 is 0.036. In other words, there was a statistically significant difference between the two proportions at the five per cent level ($p<0.05$), but not at the one per cent level ($p<0.01$).

The effect of small numbers

The calculations above rely on the assumption that a sample proportion has an approximately Normal distribution in large samples (Altman, 1991). It is reasonable to use this approximation when the proportion (using a particular drug, for example) multiplied by the sample size (i.e. those answering the question on use of that particular drug) is greater than five. This becomes important for the less commonly used drugs, such as heroin, and for drugs whose use was less prevalent in earlier sweeps of the BCS, such as cocaine. Where the assumption has been violated, the statistical test outlined above was not performed and a non-significant result presented.

Design effects

The 2000 BCS core sample was designed to give, after appropriate weighting, both a representative cross-sample of private households in England and Wales, and of individuals aged 16 or over living in them. The small user Postcode Address File (PAF) was used as the sampling frame. The sample was clustered, with sampling points being quarter postcode sectors. The sample was also stratified by police force area with the aim of ensuring that there were at least 300 interviews per police force area. The main rationale for clustering was that the logistics of face-to-face interviewing would be very costly (mainly in terms of travel time) if interviewers had to interview a totally unclustered sample. The stratification on police force area induces some clustering, but it is the selection of sample points (made up of an average of a little over 20 respondents) that induces most of the design effect. For more details of the sample design, see Hales *et al.* (2000).

Due to the stratification and clustering of the BCS sample design, a design factor has to be used when calculating significance tests – they cannot be calculated on the assumption of a simple random design. This is done by calculating the effect of the sample design (design effect) on the errors associated with the estimates of different types of drug use among various groups. There is a trade-off between levels of clustering in the sample design and the margins of error for estimates. This is why it is usual for design effects to be greater than one, meaning that the errors are proportionally larger. Occasionally, a design effect will be less than one and in this case, the sampling errors may in fact be slightly smaller than they would otherwise have been had a simple random sample been employed.

Design effects relating to the 1998 and 2000 BCS were only calculated for each question in the drugs self-completion component for the full 16 to 59 age range and not for any sub-groups. These are used in the tests in this report where 1998 and 2000 data are presented. However, a fuller set of design effects are available for specific age groups (16–19, 20–24, 25–29, 16–24 and 16–29) and their responses to individual drugs questions for 1994 and 1996, and these were used where appropriate. This full set of design effects is available from the authors on request, but, as a guide, design effects for the complete range of 16- to 59-year-olds for each drug and for each year are set out in Appendix D in Table D.1.

Appendix F   The questionnaire

(1) Whether respondent has heard of various drugs

[The possible responses to all 13 questions in this section were (1) Yes; (2) No.]

Have you HEARD of AMPHETAMINES (SPEED, WHIZ, UPPERS)?
Have you HEARD of CANNABIS (MARIJUANA, GRASS, HASH, GANJA, BLOW, DRAW, SKUNK)?
Have you HEARD of COCAINE/COKE?
Have you HEARD of CRACK/ROCK/STONES?
Have you HEARD of ECSTASY ('E')?
Have you HEARD of HEROIN (SMACK, SKAG, 'H')?
Have you HEARD of LSD or ACID?
Have you HEARD of MAGIC MUSHROOMS?
Have you HEARD of METHADONE or PHYSEPTONE?
Have you HEARD of SEMERON?
Have you HEARD of TRANQUILLISERS (TEMAZEPAM, VALIUM)?
Have you HEARD of AMYL NITRITE (POPPERS)?
Have you HEARD of ANABOLIC STEROIDS (STEROIDS)?

(2) Whether respondent has ever taken various drugs

[The possible responses to all 17 questions in this section were
(1) Yes; (2) No; (3) Don't want to answer.]

[N.B. The respondent is only asked about those drugs which he/she has heard of.]

Have you EVER taken AMPHETAMINES (SPEED, WHIZ, UPPERS)?
Have you EVER taken CANNABIS (MARIJUANA, GRASS, HASH, GANJA, BLOW, DRAW, SKUNK)?
Have you EVER taken COCAINE/COKE?
Have you EVER taken CRACK/ROCK/STONES?
Have you EVER taken ECSTASY ('E')?
Have you EVER taken HEROIN (SMACK, SKAG, 'H')?

Have you EVER taken LSD or ACID?

Have you EVER taken MAGIC MUSHROOMS?

Have you EVER taken METHADONE or PHYSEPTONE?

Have you EVER taken SEMERON?

Have you EVER taken TRANQUILLISERS (TEMAZEPAM, VALIUM)?

Have you EVER taken AMYL NITRITE (POPPERS)?

Have you EVER taken ANABOLIC STEROIDS (STEROIDS)?

Have you EVER taken GLUES, GAS OR AEROSOLS (TO SNIFF OR INHALE)?

Apart from anything you have already mentioned, have you EVER taken PILLS OR POWDERS (not prescribed by a doctor) when you didn't know what they were?

Apart from anything you have already mentioned, have you EVER SMOKED SOMETHING (excluding tobacco) when you didn't know what it was?

Apart from anything else you have already mentioned, have you EVER taken ANYTHING ELSE THAT YOU THOUGHT WAS A DRUG (not prescribed by a doctor) when you didn't know what it was?

The same list of drugs are used in the next two questions:

(3) Whether respondent has taken drugs in last 12 months

(4) Whether respondent has taken drugs in the last month

References

ACMD (Advisory Council on the Misuse of Drugs) (1998). *Drug Misuse and the Environment.* London: Stationery Office.

Altman, D. (1991). *Practical Statistics for Medical Research.* London: Chapman and Hall.

Balding, J. (2000). *Young People and Illegal Drugs into 2000.* Exeter: Schools Health Education Unit.

Bean, P. (1993). *Cocaine and Crack: supply and use.* Hampshire: Macmillan Press.

Bennett, T. (2000). *Drugs and Crime: the results of the second developmental stage of the NEW-ADAM programme.* Home Office Research Study 205. London: Home Office.

Bless, R., Korf, D., Riper, H. and Diemel, S. (1997). *Improving the Comparability of General Population Surveys on Drug Use in the European Union: final report.* Amsterdam: Amsterdam Bureau of Social Research and Statistics.

Boys, A., Dobson, J., Marsden, J. and Strang, J. (2001). *Cocaine Trends: a qualitative study of young people and cocaine use.* London: National Addiction Centre.

CACI (1993). ACORN *User Guide.* London: CACI.

Collin, M. (1997). *Altered State: the story of ecstasy culture and acid house.* London: Serpent's Tail.

Corkery, J.M. (2000). 'Snowed under: is it the real thing?' *Druglink,* May/June 2000.

Corkery, J.M. (2001). *Drug Seizure and Offender Statistics, United Kingdom, 1999.* Statistical Bulletin 5/01. London: Home Office.

Department of Health (1996). *Health Survey for England 1996.* London: Department of Health. <www.official-documents.co.uk/document/doh/survey96/ehch8.htm>

Department of Health (1999). Statistics on Alcohol: 1976 onwards. London: Department of Health. <www.doh.gov.uk/public/sb9924.htm>

Department of Health (2000). *Statistics from the Regional Drug Misuse Databases for six months ending March 2000.* London: Department of Health.

Ditton, J. and Frischer, M. (2001). 'Computerised projection of future heroin epidemics: a necessity for the 21st century?' *Journal of Substance Use and Misuse,* 36(1-2): 151-166.

Ferrence, R. (2001). 'Diffusion theory and drug use.' *Addiction,* 96(1), 165-173.

Flood-Page, C., Campbell, S., Harrington, V. and Miller, J. (2000). *Youth Crime: findings from the 1998/99 Youth Lifestyles Survey.* Home Office Research Study 209. London: Home Office.

Goddard, E. and Higgins, V. (2000). *Drug use, smoking and drinking among young teenagers in 1999.* London: The Stationery Office.

Gore, S. and Drugs Survey Investigators' Consortium (1999) 'Effective monitoring of young people's use of illegal drugs: meta-analysis of UK trends and recommendations.' *British Journal of Criminology,* 39(4), 575-584.

Gossop, M., Griffiths, P., Powis, B. and Strang, J. (1994). 'Cocaine: patterns of use, route of administration and severity of dependence.' *British Journal of Psychiatry,* 164: 660-664.

Goulden, C. and Sondhi, A. (2001). *At the Margins: drug use by vulnerable young people in the 1998/99 Youth Lifestyles Survey.* Home Office Research Study (forthcoming).

Graham, J. and Bowling, B. (1995). *Young People and Crime.* Home Office Research Study 145. London: Home Office.

Hague, L., Willis, M. and Power, M. (2000). *Experience of Drug Misuse: findings from the 1998 Northern Ireland Crime Survey.* Northern Ireland Office Research and Statistical Bulletin 4/2000.

Hales, J., Henderson, L., Collins, D., Becher, H. (2000). *2000 British Crime Survey (England and Wales): technical report.* London: National Centre for Social Research.

Haynes, G., Bottomley, T. and Gray, A. (2000). *National Crack Cocaine Treatment and Response Strategy: minimum and maximum requirements for effective practice and service development.* Department of Health Advisory Document to the UKADCU. <www.drugs.gov.uk/national_crack_strategy.pdf>

Hunt, L. and Chambers, C. (1976). *The Heroin Epidemics: a study of heroin use in the United States, 1965-75*. New York: Spectrum.

Kershaw, C, Budd, T., Kinshott, G., Mattinson, J., Mayhew, P. and Myhill, A. (2000). *The 2000 British Crime Survey (England and Wales)*. Home Office Statistical Bulletin 18/00. London: Home Office.

Leitner, M., Shapland, J. and Wiles, P. (1993). *Drug Usage and Drugs Prevention*. London: The Stationery Office.

MacDonald, Z. and Pudney, S. (2000). 'Illicit drug use, unemployment and occupational attainment.' *Journal of Health Economics,* 19(6): 1089-1115.

McNeill, A. and Raw, M. (1997). *Drug Use in England: results of the 1995 National Drugs Campaign Survey*. London: Health Education Authority.

Measham, F., Parker, H. and Aldrige, J. (1998). Starting, Switching, Slowing and Stopping: report for the Drugs Prevention Initiative integrated programme, *DPI Paper 21*. London: Home Office.

Miller, P. and Plant, M. (1996). 'Drinking, smoking and illicit drug use among 15 and 16 year olds in the United Kingdom.' *British Medical Journal,* 313(7054): 394-397.

Miller, P. and Plant, M. (2000). 'Drug use has declined among teenagers in United Kingdom.' *British Medical Journal,* 320(7248): 1536-7.

Parker, H., Aldridge, J. and Measham, F. (1998). *Illegal Leisure: the normalisation of adolescent recreational drug use*. London: Routledge.

Pearson, G. (1998). *Normal Risks: an ethnographic study of adult recreational drug use in inner London*. Conference paper, 9th Annual Conference on Drug Use and Drug Policy, Palma, Spain.

Pearson, G. and Gilman, M. (1994). 'Local and regional variations in drug misuse: the British heroin epidemic of the 1980s', in Strang, J. and Gossop, M. (Eds.). *Heroin Addiction and Drug Policy: the British system*. Oxford: Oxford Medical Publications.

Pearson, G. and Patel, K. (1998).'Drugs, deprivation, and ethnicity: outreach among Asian drug users in a northern English city.' *Journal of Drug Issues,* 28(1), 199-224.

Ramsay, M. (1999) 'New perspectives on drugs surveys: comments on articles by Sheila Gore and Ziggy MacDonald.' *British Journal of Criminology*, 39(4), 648-651.

Ramsay, M. and Partridge, S. (1999). *Drug Misuse Declared in 1998: results from the British Crime Survey.* Home Office Research Study 197. London: Home Office.

Ramsay, M. and Percy, A. (1996). *Drug Misuse Declared: results of the 1994 British Crime Survey.* Home Office Research Study 151. London: Home Office.

Ramsay, M. and Percy, A. (1997). 'A national household survey of drug misuse in Britain: a decade of development.' *Addiction*, 92(8), 931-937.

Ramsay, M. and Spiller, J. (1997). *Drug Misuse Declared in 1996: latest results from the British Crime Survey.* Home Office Research Study 172. London: Home Office.

SAMHSA, Office of Applied Studies (2000). *Summary of findings from the 1999 National Household Survey on Drug Abuse.* Rockville, Maryland: Substance Abuse and Mental Health Services Administration, Office of Applied Studies.

Shiner, M. and Newburn, T. (1997). 'Definitely, maybe not: the normalisation of recreational drug use among young people', *Sociology*, 31(3), 1-19.

Shiner, M. and Newburn, T. (1998). 'Taking tea with Noel: the place and meaning of drug use in everyday life', in: South, N. (Ed.), *Drugs: cultures, controls and everyday life*, 139-159. Thousand Oaks: Sage.

Sondhi, A., Hickman, M. and Madden, P. (1999). *Asian Heroin Smoking.* Short Report No.3. London: Imperial College, CRDHB.

Tasker, T., Raw, M., McNeill, A., O'Muircheartaigh, C., Bowden, C. and Heuston, J. (1999). *Drug Use in England: results of the 1996 National Drugs Campaign Survey.* London: Health Education Authority.

The Women's Unit (2001). *Individual Income 1996/97-1998/99.* London: Cabinet Office. <www.womens-unit.gov.uk/publications.htm>

UKADCU (United Kingdom Anti-Drugs Co-ordination Unit) (2000). *Second National Plan.* London: Cabinet Office.

UKADCU (United Kingdom Anti-Drugs Co-ordination Unit) (2001). *United Kingdom Anti-Drugs Co-ordinator's Annual Report 2000/01: a report on progress since 2000 of the Government's ten-year anti-drugs strategy.* London: Cabinet Office.

Wade, G. and Barnett, T. (1999). 'Homelessness, Drugs and Young People' in Marlow, A. and Pearson, G. (Eds.) *Young People, Drugs and Community Safety.* Dorset: Russell House Publishing.

White, A. and Malbon, G. (1995) *1994 British Crime Survey Technical Report.* Unpublished report by OPCS.

White, C. and Lewis, J. (1998). *Following up the British Crime Survey 1996: a qualitative study.* London: SCPR.

Wish, E.D., Hoffman, J.A. and Nemes, S. (1997).'The Validity of Self-Reports of Drug Use at Treatment Admission and at Follow-Up: comparisons with urinalysis and hair assays', in Harrison, L. and Hughes, A. (Eds.) *The Validity of Self-Reported Drug Use: improving the accuracy of survey estimates.* NIDA Research Monograph 167. Rockville: NIH.

RDS Publications

Requests for Publications

Copies of our publications and a list of those currently available may be obtained from:

Home Office
Research, Development and Statistics Directorate
Communications Development Unit
Room 201, Home Office
50 Queen Anne's Gate
London SW1H 9AT
Telephone: 020 7273 2084 (answerphone outside of office hours)
Facsimile: 020 7222 0211
E-mail: publications.rds@homeoffice.gsi.gov.uk

alternatively

why not visit the RDS website at
Internet: http://www.homeoffice.gov.uk/rds/index.html

where many of our publications are available to be read on screen or downloaded for printing.